Abe
Lincoln
and the
Frontier Folk
of New Salem

Abe Lincoln

and the Frontier Folk of New Salem

Thomas P. Reep

Introduction and Editing by

Constance Reep
Unsworth

Southfarm Press, Publisher
Middletown, Connecticut

This edition is an abridged and rewritten version
of *Lincoln and New Salem* by Thomas P. Reep,
printed privately in 1918 by the Old Salem Lincoln League.
Additional material has been added.

Southfarm Press, *Publisher*
Publishing Imprint of Haan Graphic Publishing Services, Ltd.
P.O. Box 1296, Middletown, Connecticut 06457

ISBN: 0-913337-36-6

Library of Congress Cataloging-in-Publication Data
Reep, Thomas P., 1870-1960.
   Abe Lincoln and the Frontier Folk of New Salem /
Thomas P. Reep ; introduction and editing by Constance Reep Unsworth.
      p. cm.
   "This edition is an edited and rewritten version of: Lincoln and New Salem, by
Thomas P. Reep, printed privately in 1918 by the Old Salem Lincoln League, with
new material added—T.p. verso
   "In 1927 the Old Salem Lincoln League published: Lincoln at New Salem ... It was
intended to take the place of: Lincoln and New Salem"—About this book
   Includes bibliographical references and index.
   ISBN 0-913337-36-6
      1. Lincoln, Abraham, 1809-1865—Homes and haunts—Illinois—New Salem
(Menard County) 2. New Salem (Menard County)—History—19th century.
I. Unsworth, Constance Reep, 1927-II. Reep, Thomas P., 1870-1960. Lincoln at New
Salem. III. Title.

E457.35 .R3 2000
977.3'355—dc21

                                                            00-029140

Visit our web site at http://www.war-books.com

•*Contents*•

•Illustrations•

ILLUSTRATION CREDITS

All photographs, artwork and maps not specifically credited are taken from *Lincoln and New Salem,* which was privately printed in 1918. Photographs on the following pages are courtesy of Constance Reep Unsworth: 12, 90, 93. Photo on page 48 is courtesy of Donald Buckley. Photo on page 58 is by Mathew Brady and has been retouched. Courtesy of the U.S. Department of State. No source is credited for the art depicting Chief Black Hawk on page 63. Photo on page 134 is courtesy of the Meserve Collection. Photo on page 149 is from a Daguerrotype by Mathew Brady. Courtesy of the Library of Congress.

Dedicated to my grandfather
Thomas P. Reep,
*who originally researched
and wrote this book,
and to my father*
Philip T. Reep,
who preserved it.

—*Constance Reep Unsworth*

About this Book
By Constance Reep Unsworth

I have based this year 2002 book on a thin edition written by my grandfather, Thomas P. Reep, and privately printed in 1918. It was entitled *Lincoln and New Salem.*. According to an interview of my grandfather by Joseph Booton in 1934, Thomas P. Reep worked to assemble every available scrap of evidence about the town of New Salem and Lincoln's association with it for his 1918 book. There is a copy of Booton's interview with my grandfather in the Illinois State Historical Library in Springfield.

Lincoln and New Salem was not copyrighted and had replaced a small pamphlet entitled *Prospectus of The Old Salem Lincoln League for the Restoration of New Salem, the Early Home of Abraham Lincoln.*

I have only one copy of *Lincoln and New Salem.* I found it among my late father's papers. My father, Philip T. Reep, had evidently had the book rebound and had had the title and his name stamped on the cover. Inside, on the title page, he had written in pencil, "This book is the property of Philip T. Reep, formerly of Eureka College." I think he must have written this after he transferred to Westminster College, from which he graduated. Then he continued, "Open for engagements. I room at the Hotel Neskannock. Inquire of manager." As he was an aspiring professional singer who later had a successful singing career in New York City, one can only surmise that this was by way of being a youthful advertisement! My father, like my grandfather, was an interesting character.

In 1927, The Old Salem Lincoln League published *Lincoln At New Salem*, based on *Lincoln and New Salem* and expanded to include more information about the town. It was also written by my grandfather, Thomas P. Reep. It was intended to take the place of *Lincoln and New Salem*, as explained in the 1927 foreword. It was the first book copyrighted by the League and is the single most comprehensive source of local lore about New Salem.

About Thomas P. Reep
By Constance Reep Unsworth

My grandfather, Thomas P. Reep, liked to say, "It's better to be a big fish in a little pond than a little fish in a big pond." And that is what he was.

His "little pond" was Petersburg, Illinois, where he was a prominent attorney. His law office was just behind the courthouse square. It was a small brick building, and it was still standing when I visited Petersburg in the summer of 1999.

That little building had once been the family home, but after my father, Philip T. Reep, and my aunt, Alice Reep Montgomery, had grown up and left home, my grandparents moved out. In summer, they lived a few miles outside of Petersburg in a cottage they owned at Old Salem Chautauqua Park. In winter, they resided "in town" in the hotel at one corner of the courthouse square.

As a child, I visited my grandparents at Old Salem every other summer. My grandmother would travel by train to New York City, and after a short visit, would take me back with her to Petersburg.

11

(*top*) Thomas P. Reep at about 20 years of age, when
he did his research about Abraham Lincoln. (*bottom*)
Reep in later life when he was a successful lawyer.

My visits took place during the Great Depression. Apparently many of the cottages had been repossessed by banks, for the Park was practically deserted except for a couple of weeks in the middle of the summer. Then a religious group took it over for one of their camp meetings. My grandmother and grandfather referred to this group as "The Holy Rollers," but I don't remember much more about them than that they had wonderful hymn sings in the evenings, which we often attended and thoroughly enjoyed.

Across the Sangamon River from Old Salem was a site that my grandfather told me was called New Salem, and that for a number of years Abraham Lincoln, his hero, had lived there.

Much restoration was taking place at New Salem. I remember that my grandfather was very involved with this restoration as a director of the Lincoln League, and when the village had been rebuilt and New Salem was finally opened as a State Historic Site, he took me to see it and proudly showed me around.

My grandfather, my grandmother, and I attended the big banquet at which Lincoln's New Salem was dedicated. This was an exciting event—my first banquet—and it made a big impression on me, mainly because I had to wear a dress and put on shoes, which I had discarded for the better part of the summer. (Going barefoot was a huge treat for a New York City kid!)

When my grandfather was a young man, he had become interested in Lincoln's early life at New Salem. Lincoln had been dead only about five years when my grandfather was born, in 1870, about five miles west of Petersburg. As a youth, my grandfather had explored the site of the deserted village of

New Salem. When he was about 20 years old and attending college in Valparaiso, Indiana, he interviewed people around the Petersburg area who had known Lincoln during the New Salem years. He was gathering material for an article he had been asked to write for the college newspaper.

My grandfather knew that William G. Greene, who still lived near Petersburg at that time, had lived in New Salem while Lincoln lived there and had actually worked with Lincoln. Although Greene was old and got around in a wheelchair, his mind and memory were still intact. My grandfather interviewed him extensively.

In addition, my grandfather asked Greene if he knew of anyone who was still around who could take him out to the site of the village and point out where various people had lived and tell him something about them. Greene told him to look up John Watkins. Watkins took my grandfather over the site and provided him with invaluable information.

There were many things about Lincoln that my grandfather particularly admired. As a raconteur himself, Thomas Reep naturally admired Lincoln's talent in telling stories. He also admired Lincoln's physical strength and his ability to do any manual job that was given to him. Being only one generation removed from settlers of the area, my grandfather particularly respected the abilities that enabled those early settlers to accomplish the feats of physical and psychological strength that allowed them to endure.

But among the qualities Lincoln possessed, those my grandfather talked most about were Lincoln's fairness, his loyalty to his friends, and his continual identification with ordinary folk throughout his life. These were qualities that Lincoln and my grandfather shared. My grandfather, in his practice of the law, was often called upon by the less "respectable" members of the Petersburg community. He would always come to their aid, often without a fee being paid. Many is the young man my grandfather prevented from spending time in the local jail for over-indulgence in what my grandfather called "John Barleycorn." A temperate man himself, he nevertheless had sympathy for those with less self-discipline. When my grandfather reached old age and was alone (he lived to be 90), those old friends kept an eye on him, did errands for him, and made sure he came to no harm.

Then, of course, my grandfather was interested in our family's connections with Lincoln's time in New Salem. Both the Reep family and my grandmother's family, the Shipps, had ties to that period of Lincoln's life. Parthena Jane Shipp, whose name was given to her by Lincoln, was my grandmother's mother. And the Reep family was also connected with the Armstrongs of Clary's Grove, who were much involved with Abraham Lincoln during his New Salem days. My grandfather told me their stories, and you will find those stories here in this book.

I remember those summers spent with my grandparents in the cottage at Old Salem with great affection. I remember that my grandfather taught me to swim in the lake— which unfortunately is no longer there. I remember that he made sure I had a pony, which he taught me to ride during my stay, and which I'm now sure must have been a financial sacrifice. I remember that he bought me a second-hand bike and taught me to ride it. I remember eating southern fried turtle, which he had caught and which he convinced me to try by telling me that it was chicken. I remember that he was a hunter, and provided the makings for dove pie, and that he was a gardener, and provided corn on the cob daily. I remember sitting on his lap on the porch during those awesome prairie line storms, feeling quite safe while he explained about thunder and lightning. And he and his bird dog, Lady, were the ones who taught me to love dogs and to treat them with respect.

I can see now that my grandfather was trying to develop in me a degree of self-reliance unusual in a city girl during the 1930s. He sometimes chided me for being a "sissy," and frowned on giving in to little fears. He used tales of Lincoln and the pioneers as examples of independence and courage.

My grandfather would have told me not to write so much about him here—that Lincoln was the one who was important. But I beg to differ.

The influence on Lincoln of his experiences at New Salem surely did, as my grandfather says, help develop the future president's character into what it eventually became. But those kinds of influences built the character of many men and women who lived in those times, times that demanded neighborliness, reliability, toughness, and a sense of community. My grandfather was one of the last generation brought up in that rugged atmosphere at the end of the frontier era. Abraham Lincoln exemplified the values that my grandfather believed in and that he saw fast disappearing. The world changed while my grandfather was writing this book. The Great War, what we now call World War I, was raging. Nothing would be the same after that.

F oreword

New Salem, Illinois, was Abraham Lincoln's alma mater. He came to New Salem a friendless, overgrown boy, uncouth and uneducated, with a knowledge of only the barest rudiments of reading, writing, and arithmetic. During the six years of his residence in New Salem, his character was formed and his education was completed. There he acquired the name of Honest Abe, and the pathway his feet were to tread during his future life blazed ahead of him. There his great heart was broken by the loss of his first love, the one great romance and tragedy of his life.

We find, however, that many Americans have been so engrossed with other matters more personal to them, that they have failed to acquaint themselves with this character-building phase of Lincoln's life.

The love and regard of the great majority of Americans for Abraham Lincoln and their desire to honor his memory has led me to write this book. Believing that a larger and more intimate knowledge of Lincoln, particularly during the formative years of his life, will bring Americans into closer touch with him and give them a better understanding of his qualities, it has seemed fit and proper to enlarge upon his life at New Salem. It is important to show how New Salem's environment and Lincoln's experiences in that environment helped mold his character and influence his later life.

—Thomas P. Reep, 1918

1 George McClellan Compared to Bab McNabb's Rooster

One of Abraham Lincoln's most striking faculties was remembering everything that had attracted his attention and using that information in illustrating any point he desired to make. It is said that following one of General George B. McClellan's strategic retreats during the Civil War, Lincoln likened him to Bab McNabb's rooster.

General McClellan, known as Little Mac, was only 34 years old when Lincoln put him in charge of the Army of the Potomac in 1861. McClellan proved to be a vain, ambitious but overly cautious military leader. On October 10, the General said to Lincoln, "Don't let them hurry me is all I ask."

Bab McNabb was a New Salem, Illinois, "sport" in the 1830s. On a visit to Springfield he had found a very handsome fighting cock for which he traded and took home to New Salem. With Bab's connivance, word got to the Clary's Grove boys that he had a wonderful fighting cock, and a challenge to combat immediately followed. The preliminaries were agreed upon, and on the day set, the sports all gathered at the cock pit, said by local tradition to have been between the Offut store and Clary's grocery.

Betting, as usual, was brisk, and Lincoln was elected to referee the bout. The two cocks were dropped into the pit. The local bird, having absorbed some of the aggressiveness of its owner, advanced cautiously toward its opponent, upon which the much heralded stranger brought in by Bab beat a hasty retreat. In a moment, Bab's bird was running in circles around the pit.

Bab, with an expression of disgust, leaped into the pit, seized his bird, and flung it into the air. It lit on a pile of saplings that had been cut and hauled for wood, and stretching its neck and flapping its wings, crowed lustily. All eyes were on the bird when Bab, in withering tones, said, "Yes, you little s__ of a b____! You are great on dress parade, but not worth a d___n in a fight."

Judgment Day in New Salem

On another occasion during the Civil War, Lincoln again referred to his life in New Salem, according to the poet, Walt Whitman. In 1833, Lincoln had been roused from his bed by a rap at his door. A voice exclaimed, "Arise, Abraham, the day of judgment has come!" Lincoln rushed to his window and apparently saw the brilliant Leonid meteor storm of 1833. Lincoln described it as, "...the stars falling in great showers," according to Whitman.

The annual Leonid meteor show, which is particularly intense every 33 years or so, was a brilliant light event of cosmic pellets in 1833. Many people probably thought it was the end of the world.

Lincoln told a group of bankers during the Civil War about witnessing this meteor shower. The bankers were meeting with the president about the stability of the Union.

"But looking back of them [the meteor showers] in the heavens I saw all the grand old constellations with which I was so well acquainted, fixed and true in their places. Gentlemen, the world did not come to an end then, nor will the Union now."

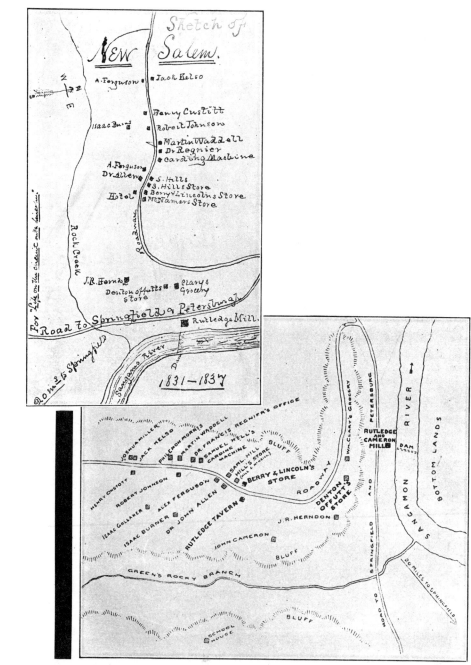

Two hand-drawn maps of New Salem, Illinois, in 1831 to 1837. The bottom map was made by J. McCan Davis in 1896. Davis was aided by former residents of New Salem in making the map.

2 *New Salem, Illinois*

The Sangamon River, winding its devious way from the southeast, bends sharply westward in its course, and striking a high bluff, is turned abruptly north. This bluff extends north and south a distance of about one-half mile with a ridge extending westward from the center, giving the impression of the letter T. Creeping around the edges of this bluff, on the north and also on the south, are two branches of the river, each of which originates near the west line of New Salem. The branch on the north runs in a northeasterly direction and the branch on the south runs first southeast and then turns slightly toward the north. Both empty into the river.

Beginning about 300 feet west of the brow of the bluff, just to the north of the high point of the ridge extending east and west, begins a hollow, fairly deep and extending northward to the north branch, making the bluff north of the center line into a ridge about 100 feet wide on the top. The main ridge toward the west, between the two branches, while slightly changing its contour, widens and merges into the level prairie.

Here John M. Cameron and his uncle, James Rutledge, settled on July 29, 1828. Previously that year, on February 8, both Cameron and Rutledge had entered claims on land a few miles farther north, the tract claimed by Rutledge being on Concord Creek where they intended to build a dam and erect a mill. However, having decided that the supply of water was insufficient at this place, and the place selected above on the Sangamon being nearer the Clary's Grove settlement and more convenient for the settlers in the east part of the county, Cameron entered the tract referred to, and he and Rutledge immediately petitioned the legislature of Illinois for the right to dam the Sangamon River. It was duly granted. This dam was built by sinking log pens side by side across the river and filling them with rock, and, it is said, the dam required more than a thousand wagon loads. The mill being double, combining a grist and saw mill, was set upon pillars made of pens of rocks, elevated above the level of the dam. It was set out some distance from the shore, the passageway thereto from the bank being made of split logs.

Contemporaneously with the construction of the mill and dam, both James Rutledge and John M. Cameron erected log cabins on the ridge extending west from the bluff and they moved there from the claims referred to above, taken by them a few miles north. On October 23, 1829, they had Reuben S. Harrison survey and lay out the town of New Salem for them in the name of John M. Cameron, who held the legal title.

Making a Town

At this time there were settlements at Clary's Grove a few miles southwest; at what is now Athens, about seven miles southeast; at Sugar Grove, some ten or twelve miles a little north of east; at Indian Point a short distance southwest of Sugar Grove; and on Concord Creek, about five miles north of New Salem. With a mill to bring these settlers to New Salem, the opportunity for business there was good, and Samuel Hill and John McNeil (his true name was McNamar) erected a building of logs and opened a store. They sold tea, coffee, sugar, salt, and whiskey in the grocery line, and blue calico, brown muslin, cotton chain and straw hats, with a few ladies' hats and other ornamental feminine apparel, in their dry goods department.

A post office was established on Christmas Day in 1829, and Samuel Hill was made postmaster. George Warburton then built a store building and put in a stock of goods, but he soon sold out to the Chrisman brothers, one of whom, Isaac P., became postmaster on November 24, 1831. William Clary, the brother of John, who had given his name to the grove where he settled in 1819, erected and became proprietor of Clary's Grocery.

Then came Dr. John Allen, who erected a dwelling across the street south from the Hill and McNamar Store. In addition to his professional duties, Dr. Allen conducted a Sunday School. An ardent temperance man, he formed the first temperance society in the community. The place of meeting was in his residence and in the log schoolhouse erected shortly before this time on the hillside south of the site of New Salem. Dr. Allen was bothered as to whether it was right or wrong to engage in the practice of his profession on Sunday, and compromised by relieving the sick, but giving his earnings on that day wholly to the work of the Lord.

Then during the summer of 1830, Henry Onstott

moved from Sugar Grove, erected a dwelling, and established a cooper's shop. He supplied kegs and barrels for the flour and meal made at the mill and to contain the cured pork shipped by flatboat to the markets of the South, generally from Beardstown to which place it was hauled in wagons.

The Town Becomes Self-Supporting

During the summer of 1831, Denton Offut, on his return from a flatboat excursion to New Orleans, contracted for Lot 14 north of Main Street and erected a store building. The deed was dated September 2nd of that year. Then came a rush of other settlers. Philemon Morris, a tanner, erected a dwelling and established a tan yard; Joshua Miller, a blacksmith and wagon maker, built a residence and established a shop; Alexander Furgeson and Peter Lukins were shoemakers; Robert Johnson, the wheelwright, made looms, spinning wheels and furniture; Martin Waddel, the hatter, made hats out of wool, rabbit fur, and the fur of other animals; the Bale family, headed by Jacob Bale, bought and operated Hill's carding machine and storehouse for wool; the Herndon brothers, storekeepers, established a store west of the James Rutledge residence and inn. In a part of the house of Joshua Miller, which was double, lived his brother-in-law, Jack Kelso, whose wife occasionally kept boarders, and who, himself, was the champion hunter and fisherman of the village.

Henry Sinco came in the fall of 1831 and sold out at the end of a year to Dr. Francis Regnier. Also came Dr. Jason Duncan, David Whery, Isaac Burner, Edmund Greer, Isaac Gollamer, and Robert and William McNeely. Caleb Carmen moved there from Rock Creek and made shoes.

On the face of the bluff looking east about 200 feet north of Clary's Grocery was an out-cropping of limestone rock, which the early settlers quarried and used to construct foundations for the houses and which they burned in lime-kilns for lime. Brick was also made on this hill out of the shale and clay found there. In fact, shale from this same stratum was later hauled to Petersburg for that purpose. A bank coal shaft or mine was opened and operated at the southeast corner of the grounds—a spring from the old shaft entrance and a gob pile still being in evidence at this writing.

Thus the town soon became self-supporting, and had it not been for the fact that it was almost inaccessible except from the west, there is no reason why the town should not have grown and become the metropolis of the county.

Four Buildings of Importance

There were four buildings in New Salem that were to be particularly associated with Abraham Lincoln.

One was the Offut store, erected on lot 14, north of Main Street on the brow of the bluff near the mill. The deed conveying this lot to Denton Offut was dated September 2nd, 1831, but in all probability was not made until after the building on the lot was erected by Offut under a verbal contract of sale. The consideration for the lot was the sum of ten dollars.

The second was the Rutledge Inn, on the west half of lots 5 and 6, south of Main street in the east part of New Salem.

The third was the Herndon Brothers' store building, in which Berry and Abraham Lincoln first "kept store." It was across the street, west of the Inn.

And the fourth was the Reuben Radford store building, occupied by Berry & Lincoln after January 15, 1833, on the west half of lot 5, on the north side of Main Street in this same part of town.

1—Rutledge and Cameron Mill
2—Lincoln's Flat Boat
3—Mill Dam
4—Ferry Boat
5—Offut Store
6—Steamboat "Utility"
7—R. J. Onstott, Born 1830
8—Rev. John Cameron's Home
9—Rutledge Tavern and Home
10—Springfield Road
11—Lincoln & Berry Grocery
12—Dr. John Allen's Res.
13—Hill & McNamer Store
14—Chrisman Bros. Store

NEW SALEM

HOME OF ABRAHAM LINCOLN 1831 to 1837

PLATTED, COPYRIGHTED AND PUBLISHED BY R. J. ONSTOTT

DRAWN BY ARTHUR L. BROWN

Adopted as Authentic by Old Salem Chautauqua Association, 1909

COPYRIGHT APPLIED FOR.   ALL RIGHTS RESERVED

LITHOGRAPHED BY J. A. FRANKS & SONS, PEORIA, ILL.

Abraham Lincoln as he appeared as a young
adult before he had his beard.

3 *The Coming of Lincoln*

The Springfield Road came up the hill from the south, between lots 4 and 5 south of Main Street in the first survey, to Main Street running east and west. Toward the west, Main Street led on to Clary's Grove. Toward the east, after a short distance, it angled toward the North, skirting the edge of the hollow indenting the north side of the ridge, passing to the west of the Offut store and north along the top of the bluff toward what is now Petersburg.

Just to the south of the Offut store, a branch road turned off, and ran down the face of the bluff in an easterly direction to the mill. This latter road was very steep and was used principally as a bridle path for the settlers to carry their grist to the mill in sacks on horseback, though occasionally some farmer would attempt it with his ox team and wagon.

There was also a road, used occasionally, which began near the intersection of the Springfield Road with Main Street and which skirted the west edge of the hollow referred to above, crossed the branch running east on the north of the ridge and shortly beyond, intersected the other road running north.

Flatboating for Offut

Abraham Lincoln was born on February 12, 1809, in what was then Hardin County in the state of Kentucky. At the age of seven years, he moved with his parents to the state of Indiana near the town of Gentryville. In February, 1830, he moved with his father's family and that of his uncle, Dennis Hanks, to Illinois and settled about ten miles west of Decatur.

Denton Offut, an embryonic Napoleon of Finance, desired to carry some produce from Beardstown to New Orleans in a flatboat, and having made inquiry in Springfield for a good man to operate the boat, learned of Dennis Hanks. It was arranged that Hanks and his nephew, Abraham Lincoln, and Lincoln's step-brother, John D. Johnston, should pilot this flatboat for Offut, leaving about the first of March, 1831. Hanks would leave them at St. Louis and go to Coles County, to which place his family was to move with Thomas Lincoln, Abraham Lincoln's father.

This was the winter of the deep snow. When the snow went off about the first of March, the country was so flooded that it was not practical to go cross-country. Consequently these men bought a row boat and floated down the river, stopping at the town of Sangamon, about seven miles northwest of Springfield. Landing here, they found Offut at Springfield and learned that he had neglected to secure a flatboat at Beardstown; so they contracted to build a boat for him out of timber to be taken from some government land near Sangamon town. By the middle of April, this boat was completed.

After loading it with barrels of cured meat, flour, wheat and other products of the country, they started on their way.

Lodged on Salem Dam

All went well until they came to New Salem, where the boat was carried by the force of the current far out on the dam. Its prow hung in the air, and its stern, into which the contents slid, was so low that the water ran into and filled that end of the boat. The boat being in a fair way of sinking, the boatmen hurriedly shifted and unloaded the boat before it sank.

The townspeople of New Salem came out in force and rendered much assistance in the way of advice. A tall, homely, raw-boned member of the crew appeared to have in mind just what to do. Borrowing an auger and preparing a wooden plug of the proper size, he bored a hole in the end of the boat that projected over the dam and by tipping that end down, caused the water to run out of the boat. Thus lightened, it slipped over the dam when the hole in the bottom of the boat was securely corked. The flatboat was then reloaded, and the boatmen proceeded on their way.

About five miles below New Salem, adjacent to Blue Lake, are what are locally known as the yellow banks on the Sangamon River. Here Squire Russell B. Godbey brought a number of hogs which he had sold to Offut for shipment to New Orleans. These stubborn porkers refused to go peaceably and quietly onto the boat. Local tradition has it that at Lincoln's suggestion, their eyes were sewn shut. As a result, the hogs walked quietly into the boat, after which the stitches were cut.

In the course of about a month, the flatboat reached

This was the type of river flatboat for hauling produce that Abraham Lincoln piloted.

The old dam at New Salem, shortly before it was cut at the east end, resulting in the washing away of the point of land shown here.

New Orleans. Lincoln and his companions, except for Dennis Hanks who had left after reaching St. Louis on the downward trip, spent a month in disposing of their stock of merchandise and seeing the sights of New Orleans.

New Orleans Slave Market

It was on this trip that Lincoln is alleged to have witnessed the sale of a family of negroes at the auction block and noted the buyer's examination of their teeth, of the shape of their bodies, and of the texture of their flesh. Overcome by the brutality of it all, Lincoln dragged his companions away and said, "If ever I get a chance to hit that thing (meaning slavery), I'll hit it hard."

Offut, having determined to establish a store at New Salem, and having employed Lincoln to clerk for him, purchased a stock of goods for shipment by boat to Beardstown, Illinois, the river port nearest to New Salem. About the middle of June, they took passage up the river. At St. Louis, Lincoln and his step-brother, John Johnston, left Offut and went to visit Lincoln's father and stepmother near Charleston, in Coles County, where they had moved from Macon County hoping to find a healthier climate.

Sometime in the latter part of July, Lincoln left for New Salem, arriving there around the first of August. On the 8th day of July, 1831, Offut had secured from the county commissioner's court of Sangamon County a license to retail merchandise at New Salem. After this, he had to secure a lot and build a store building. The building was probably erected sometime between the above date and September 2nd, at which time his deed was executed.

Lincoln Clerks at Election

While waiting for Offut, Lincoln boarded at the Rutledge Inn and "loafed" about the town. The election at that
time was held during the first week in August, and Lincoln,
being at the polling place, was asked by Mentor Graham if he
could write. Lincoln replied, "I can make a few rabbit tracks,"
whereupon he was invited to assist in keeping tally, the regular
clerk having failed to appear. It is said that during a lull in
voting, Lincoln took the opportunity to tell stories and thus
entertained and interested those present.

Of all the stories told by Lincoln on this occasion, the
one that impressed the listeners most was his famous story of
the preacher and the lizard. An itinerant preacher was dressed
in jeans pantaloons with a flap in the front held on by a single
button on his shirt, and a linsey-woolsey shirt fastened at the
collar with one button. He stepped into the pulpit and announced as his text, "I am the Christ, whom I shall represent
today." Just as he started his sermon, a small, green lizard crept
up his baggy pants leg. With one hand gesturing the strong
points of his sermon and the other seeking to stop the upward
advance of the unwelcome stranger, he continued the even
flow of his discourse. Being unable to arrest the lizard's prog-
ress, the preacher opened the button of his pantaloons, and
with one sweep and a kick, freed himself therefrom. However,
the lizard by this time, was making its way up his back.
Opening the button at his throat, he divested himself of this
garment also, the flow of his eloquence uninterruptedly march-
ing on. At this juncture, an old lady in the rear of the house
arose, pointed an accusing finger at the preacher, and said in a
piping voice, "I just want to say that if you represent Jesus

Christ, sir, then I am done with the Bible."

Lincoln's story-telling faculty and his ability to clerk at the election attracted the attention of the more prominent citizens of New Salem.

During this time, Lincoln, no doubt, assisted in the erection of Offut's store. After its completion and while waiting for the arrival of the goods to stock it, he took a job piloting the raft of one Dr. Nelson down the Sangamon River from New Salem to Beardstown on the Illinois River. Neighbors were getting too close, so Dr. Nelson was migrating to the state of Texas, where he would have more room.

Upon arriving at Beardstown, Lincoln found that the Offut goods had arrived, and starting out on foot to New Salem, he met a couple of wagons that Offut had sent for them. Offut had expected that Lincoln would wait at Beardstown for the wagons, and the drivers had been directed to hunt Lincoln up and have him look after the delivery of the goods. So Lincoln was asked to give an order for the goods, which he did, sending the wagons on back after them. He continued walking on to New Salem. Tradition has it that one of the drivers found a misspelled word in the order Lincoln had given him which he corrected. In later years, the man took much pride in telling of the incident.

From the best information we have been able to obtain, it appears that the Offut store was opened for business sometime in the middle of September, 1831. Shortly afterwards, Offut rented the mill from Cameron and Rutledge and, no doubt, had this in mind when he located the store on the brow of the hill at the fork of the roads where one branch went easterly down the bluff to the mill and the other branch turned north.

William G. Greene, from the only picture
known to exist of him as a young man. He
was Lincoln's assistant at the Offut store
at New Salem. Greene bought the Reuben
Radford store and sold the stock to Berry
& Lincoln all on the same day. He brought
Richard Yates home with him from school
at Jacksonville and took Yates to New
Salem to meet Lincoln. Greene was Collector of Internal Revenue in the Peoria, Illinois, district during Lincoln's presidency
and visited Lincoln frequently in Washington, D.C. Greene was probably the
closest personal friend Lincoln ever had.

4 *Lincoln Begins at Offut Store*

With the added duties of looking after the mill, and the further fact that money in those days was scarce and it was necessary to do a large credit business taking produce in exchange after it was raised, and with Lincoln being new to the neighborhood, it became necessary to employ an assistant who was acquainted with the financial standing and honesty of the settlers. Accordingly, William Greene, a "likely lad of eighteen years," who lived with his father, William Greene, Sr., on a farm about a mile southwest of New Salem, was employed to stay in the store with Lincoln and, as he explained to this writer, "to tell Lincoln who were good."

Offut, as his knowledge of Lincoln increased and he had occasion to note his physical prowess in feats of strength and in manly sports, came to have for him an ever increasing regard. Offut, apparently, was of the disposition that to think a thing was to talk about it, particularly when exhilarated by the juice of the corn.

So in a very short time, Offut had informed William Clary, who ran a saloon about thirty steps north of the Offut store, that Lincoln could out-run, out-lift, and throw down any man in the community. Waxing warm over his cups, Offut bet Clary ten dollars that Lincoln could out-wrestle any man they might bring against him. John (Jack) Armstrong, the champion wrestler at Clary's Grove, was selected to meet Lincoln.

When Offut told Lincoln what he had done, Lincoln at first demurred, declaring he would have nothing to do with the arrangement that Offut had made without his knowledge or consent. But when Lincoln was confronted with the alternative of wrestling or having Offut lose his bet, and knowing the impression that the locals would make of his refusal, he consented.

William Greene, Lincoln's associate in the store, was well acquainted with Armstrong's manner of wrestling and the tricks of which Armstrong was a master. Greene demonstrated many of them to Lincoln and advised him to take full advantage of his long reach by holding Armstrong at arm's length and not allowing him to get in close where he would have the advantage because of his short, powerful physique.

The Wrestling Match

On the day set for the match, which, in accord with local tradition, took place on the small square of level ground near the Offut store, the settlers came out in force. Betting ran high, from money to jackknives and treats of whiskey.

Lincoln, profiting by the warning given him by Greene, kept Armstrong at arm's length and just as strenuously did Armstrong attempt to get in close. Finding himself unable to use any of his favorite tricks that were permissible in the code of the game, Armstrong resorted to a "foul." Just what this was is more or less in dispute, but the best tradition has it that he stamped or attempted to stamp on Lincoln's instep with his boot heel, while at the same time throwing the weight of his body forward.

This act so enraged Lincoln that with his long arms and powerful shoulders, he lifted Armstrong bodily from the ground and slammed him with great force flat upon his back. Armstrong's friends assumed threatening poses and seemed about to attack Lincoln in force. Lincoln stepped back so that the building would be close behind him and braced himself for the attack.

By this time, Armstrong had recovered sufficiently to get to his feet, and stepping forward, he extended his hand to Lincoln. He apologized for his unsportsmanlike act, and in the presence of all those assembled, he acknowledged that Lincoln was the better man.

Local tradition has it that Lincoln was to wrestle with a man from Clary's Grove, run a foot race with a man from Little Grove, and fight a man from Sandridge. It is said that he out-ran the man from Little Grove, threw down the man from Clary's Grove, as set out above, and then, standing with his back to the building, told them to bring on their man from Sandridge and he would lick him "quicker than it takes a sheep to wag its tail" and that if they would allow him ten minutes breathing space between, he would lick the whole crowd.

Whatever the truth may be as to the details of this occurrence, there is no question that the wrestling match with Armstrong took place, nor is there any question but that Lincoln was victorious and that his prowess was publicly acknowledged by Armstrong, who became one of Lincoln's firmest friends and followers, as did all of Armstrong's friends and followers in the Clary's Grove settlement.

Hannah Armstrong. "Aunt Hannah," as she
was called, was born Hannah Jones in 1811.
She married John (Jack) Armstrong as a
young girl. Jack and Hannah lived at Clary's
Grove at the time Lincoln arrived in New
Salem. After Lincoln defeated Armstrong in
a wrestling match, they became good friends
and frequent companions. When out of work,
Lincoln made his principal homes at Jack
Armstrong's and Bowling Green's. Lincoln
would split wood, bring in water and entertain the children while Aunt Hannah cook-
ed meals. She mothered Lincoln, and he
later repaid her by clearing her son Duff
of a murder charge. Lincoln wasn't paid for
defending Duff, but Aunt Hannah wanted
to deed him her farm, as payment.

Clary's Grove Boys

Many writers seem to take pleasure in blackening the characters of the "Clary's Grove boys," as they were called, forgetting the fact that these men were frontiersmen living at the skirmish line on the borders of civilization. They were raised without opportunity for education or refinement, taught from their childhood and from their very environment to meet nature bare-armed and bare-breasted, and to overcome. They lived at a time when every man was his own sheriff and protected and enforced his own rights and those of his own family. Where they lived, physical prowess and sheer nerve were supreme and men were unacquainted with fear.

In accordance with the standards of their time, they were men standing upon their own feet, four-square with the world, as ready for a fight as a frolic, quick to discern streaks of yellow in men and as quick to discover and respect manhood and courage. Their virtues were many. Warm hearted and sympathetic to a fault, they ministered bountifully to every case of genuine suffering. They were always ready to lend a helping hand to a friend or neighbor, and they would share their last crust with anyone more needy than they. They hated sham and pretention and would not endure hypocrisy. They were great souled, courageous men, yet to one in distress they were as sympathetic and tender-hearted as a woman.

The wrestling incident narrated above, which occurred shortly after Lincoln took up his duties as clerk for Offut, was the start of the Clary's Grove boys' friendship for Abe Lincoln.

Shortly following the wrestling match, Lincoln's fellow clerk, Greene, complained of having lost a number of small bets on a game that a man named Estep worked by twisting the fingers of his hand together in a confusing way and challenging the onlooker to pick out the little finger. Lincoln advised Greene to bet Estep that he (Lincoln) could lift a barrel of whiskey from the floor and hold it while he took a drink out of the bung hole.

Accordingly, Greene set out in search of Estep, bent upon winning back his losses, and soon succeeded in making his bet. The stake was a fur hat. Lincoln won the bet for Greene by sitting in a squatting position and rolling the barrel upon his knees until the bung hole was opposite his face. He reached over and, gradually tilting the barrel, took a drink, which he immediately spat out.

Greene, who probably desired to credit Lincoln with some of his own shrewdness, claimed that, at Lincoln's suggestion, when he went to make the bet with Estep, he took up a small keg of liquor and holding it up in front of himself, drank out of the bung hole, declaring that Lincoln could lift a barrel and take a drink the same way, leaving Estep to assume that Lincoln was to lift the barrel in the same manner.

Soon Lincoln became the judge for the Clary's Grove boys in their horse races and physical contests, and the umpire in the settlement of their disputes. If anyone questioned Lincoln's decisions, the first mutter of criticism resulted in the fierce condemnation of the questioner by his fellows.

The Clary's Grove boys were sportsmen in the truest sense of the word. When they lost, they pocketed their loss bravely, were "game to the core" and did not hold resentment or malice against the winner. Their friendship for Lincoln made it possible for him to receive all but thirteen votes of the two hundred ninety cast for representative at the election in August, 1832.

It was these same Clary's Grove boys who followed Lincoln over the country in his campaign in 1834, standing always ready to fight his battles for him, ready to resent with their fists any abuse or slighting remarks about their idol. They elected him captain of their company in the Black Hawk War, and "Jack" Armstrong, called by some writers "the bully of Clary's Grove," was his sergeant.

The story is told locally that during Lincoln's second campaign for the presidency, William G. Greene visited him in Washington. Lincoln asked how his old friends of New Salem days stood in the coming election, and particularly asked about Henry Clark. Greene advised Lincoln that Clark was not talking right.

Lincoln, after a moment's thought, said: "Bill, when you get back home, go see Henry Clark and tell him I sent you. Say to him that at one time when he had a hard fight on his hands, I stood by him and now that I have a hard fight on, I want him to stand by me!"

Greene did as he was bid, and Clark, hesitating a moment as though to fully visualize the incident, looked up at Greene with a smile and said, "Tell Abe Lincoln that Henry Clark remembers, and that he and his house will stand by him!"

The incident Lincoln had referred to was a fight between Clark and Ben Wilcox, at which Lincoln was Clark's "second." After the fight was over, the principals were taken to the river and the blood washed from their bodies. Wilcox's second, John Brewer, who was not much more than half the size of Lincoln, being heady with liquor, strutted up to Lincoln and said, "Abe, my man licked yours, and I can lick you." Lincoln looked him over quizzically, and good naturedly replied, "If you will stand up in front of me, John, and have

Henry Clark. Lincoln acted as Clark's
Second in his fight with Ben Wilcox.
Later, Clark and Wilcox crossed the
river at the ferry just below Salem Dam
and fought out their differences. A
crowd watched the fight from the other
side of the river. The fight resulted in
a draw. Less than a year later, Wilcox
died, perhaps as a result of the fight.
Before his death, Wilcox sent for Clark
and had him promise to look after the
interests of his widow and children.

your outline chalked upon my body, and agree not to hit me outside of those lines, I will fight you." The circumstance and the droll ridiculousness of the answer caused such a laugh that the challenger forgot his belligerency and laughed with the crowd.

John "Jack" Armstrong's grave marker.

5 *Lincoln Studies and Joins Debating Club*

After Lincoln became settled in his job of clerking for Offut, he found that he had considerable leisure time, so he looked about for some books to improve his education. More than any other thing at that time, he desired to improve himself in the use of English. Meeting the local school master, Mentor Graham, Lincoln inquired of him where he might acquire an English grammar. He was advised that there was one in the possession of a man by the name of John Vance, who lived six miles in the country.

That evening after closing the store, it is said, Lincoln walked the six miles to Vance's house and secured the grammar, either by gift or by purchase, and brought it back with him. Then during evenings, Greene would hold the book, read the questions in it, see whether Lincoln could correctly answer them, and see whether or not he could correctly define terms, such as defining a phrase as: "A phrase is an assemblage of words, not constituting an entire proposition, but performing a distinct office in the structure of a sentence or of another phrase," and other such "clear and lucid" definitions.

William G. Greene, who was interviewed by this writer, told the following story. During Lincoln's presidency, while Greene was internal revenue collector for the Peoria district, he was called to Washington by Lincoln. Being admitted to Lincoln's office, he found William Henry Seward, Lincoln's Secretary of State, present. Lincoln, after saluting and shaking hands with Greene, turned to Seward and said, "Seward, shake hands with Bill Greene of Illinois, the man who taught me grammar." The statement embarrassed Greene, who himself knew little about grammar and in whose conversation grammatical rules were not always adhered to. Consequently, he did not engage in the conversation for fear Seward would notice his deficiencies and wonder at Lincoln's statement. Seward soon left, and when he had passed out of hearing distance, Greene turned to Lincoln and said, "Abe, what did you mean by telling Seward that I taught you grammar? Lord knows I don't know any grammar myself, much less could I teach you." Lincoln replied, "Bill, don't you recollect that when we stayed in the Offut store in New Salem, you would hold the book and see if I could give the correct definitions and accurate answers to the questions?" Greene replied, "Yes, Abe, I remember that, but that was not teaching you grammar." And Abe replied, "Bill, that was all the teaching of grammar I ever had."

However this may be, it appears that when some especially bothersome matter in his study of grammar confronted him, he went to the old school master, Mentor Graham, for assistance and received it.

Having mastered the rules and definitions of his Kirkham's grammar, he began the study of mathematics. During this time, his mind, naturally, ran upon mathematical problems, and these he discussed with his friends and visitors at the Offut store. Occasionally some visitor would create a knotty problem for Lincoln to solve, and Lincoln would often work on it the greater part of the night, his mind being so constituted that he was unable to let go of a proposition until he mastered it.

It is said that Lincoln could not carry a tune, but he could readily commit to memory the words of the songs and hymns in common use and took delight in reciting them in a sort of sing-song tone. It is remembered of him that in a song from the *Missouri Harmony* called "Legacy," he used to excite "the most uproarious, laughter" by substituting the words "old grey" for "red grape," the effect being very ludicrous. The words of the song follow:

LEGACY

When in death I shall calm recline
O bear my heart to my mistress dear,

Tell her it liv'd on smiles and wine,
Of brightest hue while it linger'd here.

Bid her not shed one tear of sorrow
To sully a heart so brilliant and light;

But balmy drops of the red grape borrow
To bathe the relict from morn till night.

First Speech and an Announcement

During the winter of 1832, a debating club was organized at New Salem with James Rutledge as president. They held regular meetings, and Lincoln was a member and regular attendant.

Robert B. Rutledge, a son of James Rutledge, in describing Lincoln's first attempt to speak at this club, says: "As he rose to speak, his tall form towered above the little assembly. Both hands were thrust down deep into the pockets of his pantaloons. A perceptible smile at once lit up the faces of the audience, for all anticipated the relation of some humorous story, but he opened up the discussion in splendid style, to the infinite astonishment of his friends. As he warmed to his subject, his hands would forsake his pockets, and would enforce his ideas by awkward gestures; but would very soon seek their resting place. He pursued the question with reason and argument so pithy and forcible that all were amazed. The president [Rutledge] at his fireside after the meeting, remarked to his wife that there was more than wit and fun in Abe's head; that he was already a fine speaker; that all he lacked was culture to enable him to reach the high destiny that he knew was in store for him. From that time Mr. Rutledge took a deeper interest in him."

Soon after this, Rutledge, as well as others of his friends, urged Lincoln to announce himself a candidate for the legislature. This he at first declined to do, saying that it was impossible for him to be elected; but when it was suggested that a canvass of the county would bring him prominently before the people and in time would do him good, he yielded to their solicitations and announced his candidacy in a printed circular dated March 6, 1832, setting out his platform and his sentiments with regard to matters of local importance. To show his humbleness and his reliance upon the common people, the paragraph ending his announcement is here given:

"Every man is said to have his peculiar ambition. Whether it be true or not, I can say for one, that I have no other so great as that of being truly esteemed of my fellow men by rendering myself worthy of their esteem. How far I shall succeed in gratifying this ambition is yet to be developed. I am young and unknown to many of you. I was born, and have ever remained, in the most humble walks of life. I have no wealth or popular relations or friends to recommend me. My case is thrown exclusively upon the independent voters of the county; and if elected, they will have conferred a favor upon me for which I shall be unremitting in my labors to compensate. But if the good people in their wisdom shall see fit to keep me in the background, I have been too familiar with disappointments to be very much chagrined."

Mentor Graham. Graham was the New
Salem schoolmaster who helped Lincoln
study grammar and mathematics while
in New Salem. He also helped Lincoln to
qualify as a surveyor in only six weeks.
Mentor Graham was always a good
friend of Lincoln's, but later Lincoln
had to sue him on Nancy Green's be-
half concerning a note Graham owed
to Nancy, Bowling Green's widow.

6 *Honest Abe*

About this time, it became apparent to Lincoln that Offut was nearing the end of his career as a merchant. He appears to have had other interests at other places, being a sort of "Captain of Finance," and he spread his resources so thinly that he failed. Gathering together such funds as he could lay his hands on, Offut fled the country, leaving his creditors to make what they could from the stock left.

During the time that Lincoln kept the Offut store, he found, on one occasion, that in making change, he had taken out six and one-fourth cents too much. After closing that evening, he walked three miles to return the money. On another occasion, just before closing one evening he weighed out half a pound of tea for a customer. In the morning, he found a four ounce weight on the scales. It occurred to him that his patron of the evening before had received four ounces less tea than she had paid for. He weighed up this amount of tea, closed the store, and hurried to the lady's home to correct the error.

From these incidents, and the fact of his fairness in refereeing sports and settling disputes and difficulties, he acquired the name of "Honest Abe," which followed him for the remainder of his life.

Lincoln Pilots Talisman

During the winter of 1832, it was announced in the Springfield paper that one Captain Vincent Bogue, who owned and operated a flour mill at Sangamon town near Springfield, Illinois, had chartered the steamboat *Talisman* and would make a trip with it from Cincinnati, Ohio, to Springfield as soon as the ice went out that spring and would thus prove that the Sangamon River was navigable. This was at the time when Lincoln was distributing his handbills announcing his candidacy for the legislature. Enthusiasm was running high, and the trip of this boat was a source of current and enthusiastic conversation.

A paper for the raising of funds by subscription was circulated, and the prominent settlers and business men, together with the politicians, journeyed overland to Beardstown to meet this boat. Among these was Lincoln, the most experienced navigator of the Sangamon, having already made two trips down the river as a pilot of flatboats. Lincoln piloted this boat up the river, having under his guidance a number of men armed with long-handled axes with which to clear the channel of drifts and to cut the over-hanging trees limbs.

Upon arriving at New Salem, the procession was joined by a number of additional members and went on up the river, stopping at the point nearest Springfield. Here the goods the boat had been carrying were unloaded, and the members of the expedition marched in triumphal procession to attend a great reception provided for them by the citizens of Springfield. In all these activities, Lincoln took a prominent part.

In a short time the receding waters of the Sangamon River showed the necessity of the boat's return, and accordingly the boat, with its crew and a number of persons living between Springfield and Beardstown, started back with Lincoln as pilot. When it arrived at New Salem, the boat was unable to get over the dam without the removal of a part of the dam to allow for its passage.

A dispute immediately arose between the owners of the dam and the crew of the boat, the latter claiming that the stream was navigable and therefore had been unlawfully dammed, while the proprietors claimed that they had received permission to erect their dam and were entitled to have it remain intact. However, the dispute was finally settled by compromise, and a section of the dam was removed. It was immediately replaced after the passage of the boat. Lincoln continued as pilot as far as Beardstown, from which point he made his way back to New Salem.

In 1836, another steamboat, the *Utility*, came up the river, but the water was so low when the boat reached New Salem that no attempt was made to go farther. As the water was then too low for the boat to go back, it tied up below the New Salem dam and was later sold to Colonel John Taylor and taken to Petersburg. He built a frame house out of the lumber in the boat, and used the glass for windows—the first glass windows in town—and made the first steam mill in the county with the boat's engine.

William Henry Seward, 1801-1872.
Seward was Secretary of State under
both Presidents Lincoln and Andrew
Johnson. Seward was responsible for
the U. S. purchase of Alaska from
Russia. At the time, the purchase was
referred to as "Seward's Folly."

7 *Lincoln Out of Work*

The Offut store having "petered out," as expressed by Lincoln, he found himself out of a job. Here came a turning point in his life. The question for him was whether to remain at New Salem, picking up such odd jobs of labor as he could find, or to seek "fields afresh and pastures new." On a day in April, a messenger rode into New Salem and posted and scattered about the stores a proclamation from Governor Reynolds calling upon the militia of this section of the state to rendezvous at Beardstown on April 22nd in order to put down the uprising of the tribe of Sacs Indians under Chief Black Hawk.

Previous to this time, Lincoln had become a member of the militia and had been elected captain of the New Salem company, which had been accustomed to meeting for drill twice a year. Every able-bodied male inhabitant under the laws of the state was regarded as a member and was required to meet for drill, under penalty of a fine of one dollar. Dollars being scarce articles in those days, it is needless to say that there were no slackers.

Black Hawk War

Upon reading this proclamation, Lincoln immediately seized paper and his quill pen and, making an appropriate heading at the top of the sheet, signed the same and invited others to join him in raising a company. It seems that one Kirkpatrick, who was the owner and operator of a sawmill a few miles up the river from New Salem, was at the same time busy along the same line and had arranged for a meeting of volunteers at Richland, a few miles south of New Salem.

Here these volunteers met. A temporary muster roll was made out and officers tentatively elected. Kirkpatrick was ambitious to be captain; but the Clary's Grove boys, who knew of a difficulty that had occurred some time before between Lincoln and Kirkpatrick, determined to rebuke Kirkpatrick for what they said was a dirty trick and to choose as their leader their friend and idol, Abe Lincoln.

William G. Greene, who was a member of the company, in describing the manner of this election to this writer, said: "Lincoln's friends, of whom I was one, got their heads together and decided to elect Abe captain. At one time, Abe had been employed by Kirkpatrick for a few days to move some saw logs. It was customary then, in moving logs, to have what was called cant hooks, and Kirkpatrick was to furnish one of these. When Lincoln was ready to start the work, this hook had not been furnished. Kirkpatrick agreed that if Lincoln would move the logs without it, he would pay him $2 additional at the end of the job, which is what the cant hook would have cost. But when the job was completed Kirkpatrick refused to do this.

"So the Clary's Grove boys would have none of him. Quietly circulating among the crowd, they spread their propaganda until assured of a clear majority in Abe's favor, and when the time came for the election of their captain, it was suggested and agreed that Kirkpatrick and Lincoln should step out to the front, facing in the same direction, a short distance apart, and all those favoring Kirkpatrick for captain should fall in behind him, and those favoring Lincoln should line up behind Lincoln. This was done, and Lincoln's line was twice as long as Kirkpatrick's."

These men, after agreeing upon the things necessary to take along, parted to meet at Beardstown, where the election of Lincoln as captain was officially confirmed by the company on the 21st day of April, 1832. It is interesting to note that John (Jack) Armstrong, with whom Lincoln had wrestled, was Lincoln's first sergeant in this company. They became part of the Fourth Regiment of mounted volunteers in General Samuel Whiteside's brigade, and went from Beardstown to Rock Island, thence up the Rock River to a point near Rockford, and thence south to Ottawa. Their term of enlistment having ended, the company was disbanded there on May 27th, 1832. Lincoln immediately re-enlisted as a private in Captain Alexander White's company, where his name appears upon the roll as of May 26th, the day previous to their being mustered out.

For some reason, Lincoln did not go on with this company, but appears to have enrolled in Captain Elijah Iles' company as of May 27th. This enlistment was for 20 days, and on June 16th, the company was mustered out. On the same day Lincoln re-enlisted in Captain Jacob M. Earley's company and was mustered out July 10th, 1832, at Whitewater, Wisconsin.

On the preceding night, Lincoln's horse had been stolen and he was obliged to walk from Whitewater to Peoria except when given a lift by some of his more fortunate companions. At Peoria, Lincoln and a companion, probably John T. Stuart of Springfield, bought a canoe and paddled down the Illinois River to Havana, where they sold the canoe and walked cross-country to New Salem.

Lincoln's knowledge of military maneuvers was limited, and it is said that on one occasion, being compelled to pass through a narrow gate with his company, and being unable to think of the proper command for that purpose, he said, "This company will disband and immediately fall in again inside this gate."

On another occasion, a friendly Indian who had been given a pass by General Lewis Cass came into camp, and Lincoln's men determined to kill him. Lincoln, learning what was afoot, pushed the helpless Indian behind him, and by entreaty and threat, stayed their hands and saved the Indian's life.

At another time, Lincoln violated an order of his superior officer by firing a gun within 50 yards of camp. He was arrested and deprived of his sword for a day.

Again, one of his men got into the officers' quarters and helped himself to a quantity of liquor and distributed it among his friends. The next morning, Lincoln had but a handful of men sober enough to march, and the balance were left to come on after becoming sober. Lincoln knew nothing about their taking the liquor, but he was arrested and required to wear a wooden sword for two days.

Chief Black Hawk. Born about 1767, he died on a small Indian reservation in Davis County, Iowa, in 1838. Captured with most of his Sac (Sauk) tribe in 1833, he was eventually transferred to the Iowa reservation. He was not a chief by birth, but earned his position. The Black Hawk War resulted from the actions of white squatters, who interfered with the Sac Indians' right to hunt and raise corn on land the Indians had transferred to the government. According to the treaty, the Indians had a right to use the land until it was surveyed and sold to settlers. The squatters disregarded the treaty and the Black Hawk War resulted.

Lincoln Part of Burying Detail

During this war, the nearest Lincoln got to any battle was at Kellogg's Grove on June 25th, at which place he arrived shortly after the skirmish and helped to bury the five men who had been killed by the Indians. Speaking of this in later years, Lincoln said, "I remember just how those men looked as we rode up the little hill where their camp was. The red light of the morning sun was streaming upon them as they lay heads towards us on the ground. And every man had a round, red spot on top of his head, about as big as a dollar where the redskins had taken his scalp. It was frightful, but it was grotesque; and the red sunlight seemed to paint everything all over. I remember that one man had on buckskin breeches."

Lincoln's staying the war out was not actuated wholly by patriotism, nor did he ever claim there was any particular danger from this warfare other than the hardship entailed thereby. He had no job to go back to at New Salem and nothing in view that he found more enticing or instructive than serving in this war. In each of these companies were a number of Sangamon County residents whose acquaintance he cultivated and with one of whom, John T. Stuart, a rising young lawyer of Springfield, he established an intimate friendship. This friendship endured throughout the remainder of his life, and his adoption of the law as a profession was materially influenced by this friend.

8 *Lincoln Returns to New Salem*

Upon his return to New Salem, which occurred sometime in the last days of July, 1832, Lincoln entered into his campaign for the legislature again, the election taking place on August the 6th. Lincoln was a Whig, a Henry Clay man, and the county was strongly Democratic.

However, the Democrats at New Salem were Lincoln's friends, and accompanied by a number of these—usually a squad of the Clary's Grove boys—Lincoln started out to canvass the county as fully as possible in the short time remaining. His first political speech was made after a sale at the village of Pappsville. While he was speaking, a fight broke out in the audience. Observing that one of his friends was being worsted, Lincoln leaped from the stand, seized the enemy, and lifting him bodily, slung him flat upon the ground. Then remounting the platform, he finished his speech.

Physical prowess, the exhibition of great strength, and the courage to back it up appealed to the voters of that day more than words. Lincoln's act in defense of his friend and supporter did more for him than any speech he might have made.

During this campaign, he spoke at Springfield with Major John Stuart, whom he had met in the Black Hawk War and who was a candidate for the general assembly on the same ticket as Lincoln. Lincoln's speech attracted to him the leading men of Springfield, many of whom became his fast friends and followers in later life.

Lincoln's First Election Results

Peter Cartwright, an itinerant Methodist preacher and also an experienced politician, was Lincoln's opponent, and defeated him in this election. (Cartwright was in turn defeated for Congress by Lincoln in 1846.) However, out of 290 votes cast for members of the legislature at New Salem that year, Lincoln received 277, which indicates his standing among those who knew him best. Later, Lincoln said that this was the only time during his life when he was defeated by direct vote of the people.

The experiences of this campaign, his acquaintanceship with and encouragement from Stuart, Judge Logan and Butler at Springfield, and the manner in which his New Salem friends stood by him, encouraged Lincoln to remain in the county and to try his political fortune again. In the meantime, it was necessary that he should have some employment, a means of livelihood, preferably at a place and under conditions where he could meet and mingle with the people; so he sought employment as a clerk in a New Salem store.

Nothing of this kind was offered. Then one of the Herndon brothers sold his half interest in a store the brothers owned in New Salem to William F. Berry. Rowan Herndon, the other partner, being dissatisfied with Berry, then sold his

Interest in the store to Lincoln, taking his promissory note in payment of the purchase price. Thus Lincoln, for the first time in his life, became a merchant in his own right and one of the business fraternity of the village.

A short time before this, the Chrisman brothers' business had failed and a portion of their stock of groceries had been taken over by James Rutledge in payment of a debt. This stock was purchased from Rutledge by Berry & Lincoln, they giving their note in payment. A few months later, probably in January, 1833, Reuben Radford incurred the enmity of the Clary's Grove boys, which resulted in Berry & Lincoln securing his stock of goods and moving into Radford's store.

No More than Two Drinks of Liquor

The circumstance was as follows: Radford was a large man of great physical strength, and he announced his ability to look after his own rights and to protect them. He was told that such an attitude would cause the Clary's Grove boys to try him out and they would surely "lick" him; if one couldn't, then two or three together could and would. On the day in question, Radford left his younger brother in charge of the store, admonishing him to be careful, and directing him to sell the Clary's Grove boys, in case any of them came in, only two drinks of liquor each. Sure enough, the Clary's Grove boys came and in peace got their two drinks of liquor.

Being denied more, they shoved the protesting youth out of their way, stepped behind the counter, and proceeded to help themselves, with the result that they all got rip-roaring drunk and turned things in the store topsy-turvy, broke the crockery and knocked out the windows, leaving chaos and ruin in their wake. Then they leaped on their horses and, yelling wildly, left the town for their homes.

A bunch of them passed a short distance from where Radford was stopping in the country. Hearing their yells, he immediately feared the worst, and leaping on his horse, galloped all the way to New Salem, where he dismounted from the panting and lathered steed and rushed into his store. Broken glass and crockery covered the floor, and the store seemed to be a total wreck.

Stepping outside, Radford declared that he would sell out to the first man who made him an offer. Just at that moment, William G. Greene, the erstwhile Offut clerk, came along, having been sent on horseback to the mill with some grist. Hearing Radford's words, be replied, "Sell out to me." Radford replied, "I will! How much will you give?" Greene rode up to the side of the store, stuck his head through a broken window, and surveyed the contents. He offered Radford $400 for the building, ground, and stock. Radford accepted.

Greene and Lincoln Conduct an Inventory

The news of the purchase traveled fast in New Salem. Soon Lincoln came over to see Greene, his old friend and new competitor. Looking over the contents, Lincoln announced that they must take an inventory. Greene, not understanding the term and guessing that it might mean some sort of a jamboree or celebration along the lines followed by the Clary's Grove boys just before, replied, "Abe, I don't believe this store will stand another one just at this time."

Lincoln explained that by inventory he meant listing

the goods and setting its value opposite each item. So they at once proceeded to make the inventory. Greene paid Radford $23 cash and for the balance gave two promissory notes for $188.50, which were secured by a mortgage drawn and witnessed by Lincoln on the real estate, that is, the west half of lot 5 north of Main Street.

Before the inventory was completed, it was evident that the stock would run to nearly $1,200. Berry & Lincoln bought it from Greene for $750. They paid him $250 cash* in silver dollars, assumed the payment of his notes for $377 to Radford, and turned over a horse, saddle and bridle owned by Berry for the remainder. Berry & Lincoln then moved their stock into the new store building and bid fair to make considerable money, as competition had now been reduced to one other store, the Hill & McNamar store, now owned by Hill, who, about this time, had bought McNamar's interest.

*In later life William G. Greene took delight in telling of his experience at home on the night of his purchase of the Radford Store and stock. He had sent a boy home with the meal his father had sent him after, and this boy had carried the news of Billy's purchase. The taking of the inventory and fixing of the papers covering the purchase from Radford and the sale to Berry & Lincoln kept young Greene till quite late that night, and when he arrived home the family had retired. His father, however, was awake, waiting for him. When young Greene stepped into the fireplace room where his parents slept, Greene, Sr., said: "So, Billy, you are a merchant are ye? You git along to bed and in the morning I will thrash the merchant out of you mighty quick." Young Bill held his peace until he had stirred up the coals and lighted the room with fresh kindling. Then, reaching into his pockets, he began stacking up his silver on the floor where it could be plainly seen from his father's bed, and remarked: "Pap, I've sold out and cleared this." His father raised up for a better view, reached under the pillow for his twist of tobacco, and remarked: "I'll just take a chaw! Liz, (Billy's mother) git up and git Billy a fust rate supper. He's had a hard day's work."

Unfortunately, Berry & Lincoln's venture into the mercantile business did not bring in the returns anticipated. A considerable part of the stock purchased by them from their predecessors consisted of liquor, and Lincoln's prejudice against its sale and use hindered its disposal to an appreciable extent. Their failing circumstances gave Berry the opportunity he craved, and being the senior partner, he applied for and secured in the name of Berry & Lincoln, a license to keep a tavern, which meant solely in this case, the right to sell liquor by the drink.

This permit was granted on the 6th day of March, 1833, by the County Commissioner's court of Sangamon County. A signature on the bond in the case, while purporting to be Lincoln's, is not in his handwriting, and appears to have been written there by Berry. The bond is signed by Bowling Green as surety.

Shortly afterward, Lincoln sold his interest in the store to Berry, taking Berry's promissory notes, one of which he turned over to James Rutledge in payment for his part of the indebtedness of the firm to Rutledge.

Afterward, when Berry had sold out to the Trent brothers and they had left "between two suns," leaving their notes unpaid, and Berry had died insolvent, Lincoln offered his note to Rutledge for the amount due. This Rutledge refused, stating that he had agreed to take Berry's note for the debt of Lincoln. He proposed to keep his agreement, and said that if he failed to get his money from Berry's estate, he would lose it.

9 *Ann Rutledge*

Previous to the Black Hawk War, Lincoln boarded most of the time with Rowan Herndon and John M. Cameron. Cameron had a house full of good-looking daughters, who were second cousins to Ann Rutledge.

However strange it may appear, there had never been any suspicion or suggestion of a love affair between Lincoln and any of the Cameron girls or any other of the young ladies at New Salem up to this time.

After his return from the war, Lincoln became a boarder at the Rutledge Inn and was thrown in daily contact with the proprietor's daughter, Ann. It has been suggested that on that eventful day when his flatboat hung up on the New Salem dam, among the spectators on the river bank was Ann Rutledge, and that she was one of the magnets that drew Lincoln back to New Salem and held him there when opportunities for advancement were most adverse. There is little doubt but that Ann Rutledge was present and that she stood on the river bank and viewed the acts of Lincoln unloading and floating the boat over the dam, because the whole populace

Reverend John Cameron. Cameron had
claimed the land comprising the site
of New Salem and was joint proprietor
with his uncle, James Rutledge, of the
town and mill. Cameron raised a family
of eleven girls and one son, and Lincoln
boarded with the family for a short time
during his six years in New Salem. Cameron eventually moved to California
where he died.

of New Salem was there, if local tradition is to be credited.

Lincoln, no doubt, saw Ann Rutledge there, for she was a young lady 18 years of age and "not hard to look at." She was fair, with blue eyes; her hair was very light, verging into auburn. She was slightly built, and if there is attraction between opposites, then who can say that the homely, dark complexioned, ungainly Lincoln was not attracted from the beginning to the pleasant-faced, fair-haired girl whom he saw that day at New Salem.

Whatever motive or motives may have induced Lincoln's coming to New Salem as Offut's clerk, it is certain that, when he did come, he found Ann Rutledge betrothed to John McNeil, the partner of Hill. It also would appear that McNeil's victory had not come without opposition and that he had his partner, Hill, for a rival.

McNeil was a New Yorker of good family whose parents had been in affluent circumstances and who had been well educated in his youth. About the time the young man reached maturity, his father failed in business, so the son, John, started out alone to win his fortune, intending to return and make the last days of his parents comfortable and happy. To avoid being followed or molested by his brothers or other members of his family until be had "made his pile," as he stated, he changed his name to McNeil, his correct name being John McNamar.

At the request of the parents of Ann Rutledge, her marriage to McNeil was postponed until she should become older and complete her education. It seems that the minimum sum of money McNeil had set out to accumulate was $10,000. In the late winter or early spring of 1833, finding that he had reached his goal and longing to see his parents, and having decided to marry and settle down on a farm near New Salem, he sold his interest in the store to Hill and announced his intentions of returning to New York and bringing his parents back with him to Illinois.* When he acquainted Ann with these intentions, he also explained to her about his change of name. It was agreed between them that upon his return their marriage should be consummated.

If during this time Lincoln looked with longing eyes toward Ann Rutledge with a love in his heart for her which he could not control, no outward or overt act of his gave evidence thereof. After the departure of McNamar, Lincoln continued to board at the Rutledge Inn and was thrown into close association with Ann. Feeling as he no doubt did toward her, his heart must have bled over the hopelessness of his love when he saw the object of it happy in contemplation of her coming marriage. But his lips were sealed.

Lincoln Appointed New Salem Postmaster

About this time, Lincoln was appointed postmaster at New Salem. The office had been held previously by one of the Chrisman brothers, Isaac P., who had resigned and moved away, turning the office over to Samuel Hill, who took more interest in selling whiskey and his other goods than he did in

*It is said that Hill, who was also an aspirant for the hand of Ann Rutledge, when he learned that McNamar had won, became enraged, and making out an inventory of their joint stock, he enclosed it with an abusive letter declaring they could no longer continue as partners and offering to purchase his interest. It was this letter and inventory which had been found by a school child and handed to Lincoln, and which Lincoln took to Hill, that Hill snatched from his hand and burned. It was this document, in later years, that was twisted into a manuscript and argument of Lincoln's against Christianity.

handing people their mail. Many were the women who were required to wait while Hill supplied some customer with liquor. This habit of Hill's aroused the ire of the female patrons of the post office. Through their influence, a petition was circulated and signed asking for the appointment of Abe Lincoln as post-master. The petition was so large and his recommendations so strong that, although Lincoln was not in accord with the administration politically, he was nevertheless appointed post-master on May 7th, 1833. Thereafter, until the office ceased, he held it to the complete satisfaction of the patrons, often walking a number of miles to deliver a letter which he knew a family was anxiously awaiting.

In his capacity as postmaster, the correspondence between McNamar and Ann Rutledge passed through his hands. Thus he knew that McNamar had written to Ann shortly after he left and while on his way back to New York, and that she had replied. Then a long period elapsed with no letter from McNamar. Ann was beset with fears; the assump-tion of a false name and the reasons for it given by McNamar, which had appeared adequate at the time, now caused her to doubt. They appeared to be unreasonable and flimsy and gave rise to the direst suspicions when coupled with his failure to return or to write to her in explanation.

Finally she told her family and friends about Mc-Namar's assumed name and the reasons he gave for it. Her friends only confirmed the haunting suspicions already troub-ling her. They said his story was of the "cock and bull" variety; that it was silly and foolish; that he no doubt had changed his name on account of having killed somebody and was a fugitive from justice; or that he probably had a wife at some other place, whom he had deserted and from whom he was hiding.

James McGrady Rutledge. Rutledge was
born in Kentucky on September 29, 1814.
He was a cousin of Ann Rutledge and knew
more about her love affair with Lincoln
than anyone except Ann's brother, David.
When people insisted that Ann was really
in love with McNamar and that her death
was caused by disappointment, Rutledge
always maintained that it was Lincoln
that Ann loved. Rutledge arrived in Illinois
about 1828 with his parents and Uncle James'
family. He helped haul rock for the dam at
New Salem and logs for the Rutledge and
Cameron homes. He died In Petersburg,
Illinois, on April 10, 1899.

Lincoln Declares His Love

Knowing that no communication had come from McNamar, and believing, with the other inhabitants of the village, that McNamar would not return to fulfill his vows to Ann Rutledge, Lincoln felt that he could at last break the seal of silence placed upon his lips by his sense of honor. So when on one of their walks about the village, Ann indicated her belief in the falseness of McNamar and expressed her fast ebbing regard for him, Lincoln declared his love and urged his suit with all the longing of a long repressed passion and the gentle force of his great and sympathetic heart.

From this time on, Lincoln's principal object in life was to win the love of Ann Rutledge. At every opportunity he sought to be with her: on her way to and from school; at church; at the old well near the inn. In frequent strolls over the hills and grassy vales about New Salem, they wandered on their lovers' walks until Ann Rutledge came fully to understand the greatness of the love this simple-hearted, great-souled man offered her, and to return that love.

About this time, the Rutledge family moved from the inn to a farm near Concord, some six miles north of New Salem. An older brother, David, was attending school at Jacksonville, and he urged his sister to marry Lincoln. However, it was her desire to spend a year in college, and since Lincoln had met with disaster in his mercantile venture and was burdened by debt (he had assumed the indebtedness of the firm, amounting to $1,100), it was agreed that Ann should spend a year in school and that Lincoln should make the race again for the legislature, and if he was elected, at the end of his term, or soon after, they should be married.

"She is the very picture of Ann Rutledge." James McGrady
Rutledge insisted that the young lady shown here looked ex-
actly like his cousin, Ann Rutledge, Lincoln's love in New Salem.
The girl's father signed the following statement on his death bed:
"I noticed Mr. McGrady Rutledge at least two different times
passing the office (where this young lady was keeping books),
stopped, and looked at my daughter and thinking himself un-
noticed took side glances at her from the side. This seemed so
strange to me, from the old gentlemen, I stepped outside and
shook hands with him—thinking I would give him a chance to
say something. After speaking a few words he asked me in a
whisper who the young lady was that we had in the office.
When I told him she was my daughter, he continued: 'She is
the very picture of Ann Rutledge.'"

10 *Bowling Green Encourages Lincoln*

It is proper now to explain why Bowling Green signed the bond of Berry & Lincoln as surety, and to inquire into his relationship with Lincoln. Bowling Green had migrated from Tennessee to Illinois in the early 1820s and later settled about half a mile north of the village of New Salem at the foot of the bluff marking the western line of the Sangamon River bottom.

He had married a young lady in Tennessee by the name of Nancy Potter. In the same party with him came his mother and stepfather, Robert Armstrong, and their family—Bowling being the only child of the mother by a former marriage. From her marriage to Robert Armstrong, his mother had eight children, namely, Jesse, Rhoda, Betsy, Ryal, John (Jack), Nancy, Eliza and Hugh. All had been born in Tennessee except for Eliza, who was born in Bond County after they moved there. Bowling Green was one of the first acquaintances of Lincoln. In a short time, he became one of Lincoln's strongest admirers and friends.

Green was a very large man, weighing more than 250

Nancy Green was the wife of Bowling Green. She helped care for Lincoln following the death of Ann Rutledge. Nancy Green was born in South Carolina. She married Bowling Green in Tennessee and moved to Clary's Grove with her husband, family, and her husband's mother and stepfather, Robert Armstrong. Bowling Green was half brother of John "Jack" Armstrong and there is no known picture of him in existence. Bowling Green died suddenly in 1842 while visiting at the home of Bennett Able, a neighbor. Lincoln attended Green's funeral and escorted Nancy Green ("Aunt Nancy") to her husband's grave and back home after the service.

pounds but under six feet in height. His stomach was large and protuberant, causing him to be nicknamed "Pot." He had a beautiful complexion, his skin being smooth and as pink and white as a woman's. He took life easy and lived well, in accordance with the standard of the times. His wife, Nancy, seems to have been the business manager of the family.

Green kept open house and welcomed every stranger at the family board. He had been elected justice of the peace previous to Lincoln's arrival at New Salem and was possessed of the statutes of Illinois and a few law books that he had picked up in his capacity as justice. He was consulted by Lincoln on many small matters of statute law as it affected business affairs and the conduct thereof at New Salem. Finding Lincoln's mind keen to grasp the meaning of the legal expressions and terms Green had gained through his study of the statute laws of Indiana prior to his coming to Illinois, Green loaned Lincoln his books and encouraged him in their study. Thus Lincoln and Green became fast friends and confidants and, being of the same political faith, Green became one of Lincoln's staunchest supporters and was untiring in his efforts to secure for Lincoln political preferment.

A Barrel of Knowledge

About this time, an incident occurred that was destined to have a material influence upon Lincoln's later life. A mover, passing through New Salem, stopped in front of the Berry & Lincoln store. In his wagon there was a barrel which took up considerable room and which he asked Lincoln, who stepped to the door in answer to his hail, if he would buy. Lincoln had no use for the barrel, but following the kindly impulse of his nature, he purchased it for 50 cents and set it in a corner of the store.

Some days later, noticing the barrel and being unemployed for the moment, he emptied the contents on the floor. Among these, he found a complete copy of *Blackstone's Commentaries*, and at once became absorbed in studying them. In Lincoln's own words: "I began to read those famous works, and I had plenty of time; for during the long summer days, when the farmers were busy with their crops, my customers were few and far between. The more I read, the more intensely interested I became. Never in my whole life was my mind so thoroughly absorbed. I read until I devoured them."

Previous to this time, Lincoln had spent his leisure from the duties of keeping store in perfecting his education and in the study of Shakespeare, Burns, and the current fiction of the day, and he had loved to go fishing with Jack Kelso. Kelso was one of those peculiar, impractical geniuses—well educated, a lover of nature, with the soul of a poet and all of a poet's impracticability, who could "recite Shakespeare and Burns by the hour."

Kelso and his wife had no children. To make a living, he and his wife occasionally kept a boarder, and Jack did odd jobs at which he was exceedingly handy. He did not seek and could not keep any steady employment. He loved to fish and to hunt and could catch fish when others failed and always had his smokehouse filled with venison when winter set in.

From him Lincoln learned to appreciate and understand the finer sentiments and shades of poetical expression and so "grew in wisdom and understanding."

Penalty for Swearing

It is said that one day while a partner with Berry in the store north of Main street, Lincoln was waiting on some ladies when a young man by name of Charlie Reavis came in. After joining a group of friends sitting on a box in a corner of the store, Reavis began telling a story, punctuating it with frequent oaths. It seems he had worked for a time on a river keel boat and had acquired the habit of swearing, so that he did it unconsciously, though very proficiently.

Lincoln noticed that his lady customers were ill at ease and very much shocked and that they hurried away as soon as their shopping was done. As soon as they had gone, Lincoln stepped over to Reavis and said: "Charlie Reavis, I have spoken to you a number of times about swearing in this store in the presence of ladies and you have not heeded. Now I am going to rub the lesson in so that you will not forget again." Lincoln seized him by the arm and led him out of the store to the side of the street where there was a patch of smartweeds.* Throwing Reavis on his back and putting his foot on his breast, Lincoln grabbed up a handful of these weeds and rubbed the face, mouth and eyes of Reavis with them till he yelled for mercy and protested that if Lincoln would quit and let him up he would never swear again in the presence of ladies. But

*Smartweeds and their relatives make up one of the larger plant families, totaling about 800 species. Of 50-odd kinds widespread in the U.S., most can be found in Illinois and bear the scientific name Polygonum, meaning "many knees," because their stems have swollen knots or joints and often make zigzag bends where the leaves are attached. Many of them are pests in farmers' fields but cultivated members of this family include beets, rhubarb, and Swiss chard. Smartweed's blossoms vary in color from pale pink or purple to bright scarlet.

Lincoln told him that was not sufficient, he would have to promise to quit swearing altogether. To this, Reavis agreed, and singular as it may seem, tradition has it that he kept the promise. Soon after, Reavis joined the Methodist Church under the preaching of Peter Cartwright and became an exemplary church member and citizen.

Among the books that Lincoln had picked up or borrowed were copies of Volney's *Les Ruines* and Thomas Paine's *Age of Reason*. From these he had absorbed a taint of skepticism, which tended to lead him away from the simple faith learned at his mother's knee. However, the notion that he ever wrote an essay against Christianity which was destroyed by Samuel Hill, as claimed by William Henry Herndon in his first *Life of Lincoln* (1889), is exceedingly doubtful and not supported by the weight of evidence. This notion, not known apparently to anybody else, appears to have grown out of the burning of a letter and inventory of stock, written by Hill, which had been lost and then picked up by a school child who handed it to Lincoln. (See note on page 74.)

His Hat as Postal Bag

As postmaster, Lincoln kept up his practice of carrying letters in his hat and delivering them at the homes of his patrons, but the profits derived from the office of postmaster were slight. Postage was exceedingly high and money was scarce, so the circulation of newspapers and periodicals was very limited. The mails were delivered at New Salem twice a week, if on schedule, and were very light.

Lincoln's habit, acquired at New Salem, of carrying letters and papers in his hat clung to him in later life. Many years later, when he was a practicing lawyer in Springfield, it is reported that he apologized for failing to answer a letter promptly by explaining that when he received the letter he placed it in his old hat and buying a new one the next day, he set the old one aside and neglected to take the letter from it.

In those days, one of the perquisites of the postmaster was the privilege of reading periodicals that came to his office, and there is no doubt that Lincoln took full advantage of this opportunity. During all this time, Lincoln's acquaintance with the people became more intimate and their friendships for him stronger.

A letter to George Spears with receipt attached (shown on page 86) illustrates, more plainly than any words we might write, Lincoln's unfitness for a business career. He was so kindly disposed to his patrons that he allowed their postage accounts to run on and on, advancing the amounts owed to the government out of his meager earnings. It is only fair, however, to the memory of George Spears to explain that the money for the postage, in this case, was brought by a man who was addicted to strong drink, and Mr. Spears asked for the receipt only so that he could be sure the man had paid the money. It is a matter of pride in the family that upon receipt of Lincoln's note, Mr. Spears mounted his horse without taking the time to saddle him and rode to New Salem to apologize to Lincoln and explain that he had not meant to question Lincoln's honesty, but only wanted a receipt in order to be sure the bearer of the money had not started drinking and had forgotten to pay it.

It is certain that no hard feelings were engendered by the note upon the part of the Spears family, who were always ardent supporters and followers of Lincoln.

(*top*) Copy of a letter written by Lincoln to George Spears at New Salem in 1834. (*right*) George Spears was one of the Clary's Grove boys. He had asked Lincoln for a receipt when he paid for the postage on the *Sangamon Journal*. This resulted in Lincoln's letter shown here. Mr. Spears had explained his reason for requesting the receipt and wasn't doubting Lincoln's honesty. He was Lincoln's good friend and follower for his entire life.

11 *Finances Low, Lincoln Assumes Debts of Firm*

Lincoln, being out of employment except for the job of post-master, was unable to live from the income therefrom; so he sought odd jobs, made rails, looked after the mill, helped at the sawmill, harvested hay and grain and even helped out on occasions in other stores, particularly that of Samuel Hill. He earned barely enough for subsistence.

Just at this time, when his affairs were reaching their lowest ebb, one Pollard Simons, who lived near New Salem and who was Lincoln's friend, carried to him in the woods where he was splitting rails, the word that John Calhoun, surveyor of Sangamon County, had determined to appoint Lincoln his deputy. As Calhoun and Lincoln were opposed to one another politically, Lincoln hesitated about accepting the office. He made a visit to Calhoun in Springfield and explained his position, saying that while he would be glad to have the job and badly needed what he could earn, if accepting the job involved any surrender of his political beliefs or any curb upon his right to express them, he could not accept the appointment.

Being assured upon this point, he took the appointment,

John Calhoun. Though politically
opposed to Lincoln, John Calhoun,
who was County Surveyor of Sangamon County 1833–41, appointed
Lincoln as his deputy. Mr. Calhoun
gave Lincoln responsibility for the
north end of the county, including
New Salem. Lincoln learned of his
possibly being appointed from Pollard Simons. Mentor Graham aided
Lincoln in studying surveying.
When Lincoln reported to Mr. Calhoun for duty, he was exhausted
from preparing for the position.
Mrs. Calhoun and her 16-year-old
sister made joking remarks to Mr.
Calhoun about Lincoln's appearance
at the time. Ida Tarbell has reported
that Mr. Calhoun replied, "...for all
that, he is no common man."

and borrowing some books on surveying from Mr. Calhoun, went back to New Salem. After Lincoln took his leave, Calhoun's sister-in-law spoke about the homeliness of his new deputy and his uncouth appearance, to which Calhoun replied, "For all that, he is no common man."

After arriving at New Salem, Lincoln immediately sought out Mentor Graham, the schoolmaster. He arranged for Graham to help him over the rougher and more intricate places and delved at once into the study of the books on surveying. At every spare moment from early morning until late at night he labored.

Many evenings Graham's daughter would wake up at midnight and find Lincoln and her father sitting by the fire working over some puzzling problem. Lincoln became so obsessed with this work and so absorbed in his effort to master it that he scarcely ate his meals, and his face and carriage showed the effects of his excessive concentration and application.

Henry McHenry, who married Nancy Armstrong, "Jack's" sister, and was one of the Clary's Grove friends of Lincoln, in speaking of this period of Lincoln's life, always declared that Lincoln's excessive application in his effort to master surveying had the same effect upon him physically as a bad spree of a couple of weeks usually had on other men. Lincoln became so hollow-cheeked, red-eyed and ragged looking generally that his friends were worried, fearing a mental breakdown, and expostulated with him about it.

Lincoln Begins Surveying

In six weeks however, Lincoln believed he had mastered the subject sufficiently to begin the actual work of surveying,

Nancy (Armstrong) McHenry

and he presented himself to Calhoun ready to begin work. Calhoun assigned him to the north end of Sangamon County in which he lived. It is said that while Lincoln managed to buy (or borrow, with the privilege of purchase) a compass, he was unable to buy a chain, and for a considerable time after his appointment, he used a grapevine instead. If true, it would not detract from the correctness of his surveys, as a grapevine would not shrink or expand to any noticeable extent, and, if the measurement were correct in the first place, would do the work of the chain very well and could be rolled up and carried about almost as conveniently.

The first survey job Lincoln did of which there is any record was in January, 1834, for Russell B. Godbey. Lincoln surveyed a piece of land, for which Godbey paid him two buckskins. These skins came in handy. On his return to New Salem, he took them to Hannah Armstrong, and while he rocked the cradle and entertained the children, she faced them on his pantaloons as a protection from the briers and brush through which he was compelled to walk in making surveys.

Lincoln's work now took him into various parts of the north end of the county, but in all cases he found some friend or acquaintance made earlier with whom he stayed.

Parthena Jane Shipp, a daughter of Henry McHenry, was interviewed in her 88th year. She related an incident that occurred while Lincoln stopped with her parents, who lived near Bobtown in what is now Cass County, while on one of his surveying trips in that vicinity. Mrs. Shipp was then a child of three or four years of age, and Lincoln, taking her on his knee as was his practice with children, asked her mother the child's name. Her mother told Lincoln that the child had not been named. He then asked that he be accorded the privilege of naming her. This being granted, he announced that she should be named "Parthena Jane" after Mrs. Hill, the wife of the New Salem merchant, Samuel Hill, and his very good friend. A tradition runs in the family that the child, in reply to his announcement of her name, said, "It's a d___n pretty name."

Lincoln's friendship with Henry McHenry was close, and his confidence in McHenry's integrity and patriotism is indicated by the fact that Lincoln, during the Civil War, appointed him provost marshal of the district in which he lived.

Mrs. Shipp tells of an incident which occurred shortly after her marriage years later, while she and her first husband, Green Lamkin, lived in Richland, between Petersburg and Springfield. She was returning to the house from across the road, where she had been to doctor a sick cow, when Lincoln, with one of his own little sons, and Herndon, his law partner, drove up. Lincoln stopped his horse and, looking closely at her with a puzzled expression, asked if he did not know her. She replied that she guessed he ought to, as he had named her. A smile then lit up his face, and he said, "You are Henry McHenry's daughter, and I am going to stop and have dinner with you." She told him she did not have anything prepared, but they were welcome to what she could get for them.

Directing them where to find feed for the horse, she went in and got up as nice a dinner as she could in the short time given her. She had a pitcher of sweet milk on the table, and Herndon, who appeared to have a feverish stomach from an overdose of John Barleycorn, called for a number of helpings, saying each time, "Mother, could I have another glass of

Parthena Jane Shipp, shown towards the
end of her life. Mrs. Shipp was the
daughter of Henry McHenry and Nancy
(Armstrong) McHenry, a sister of John
"Jack" Armstrong. She was named Parthena by Lincoln in honor of Parthena
Nance, the wife of Samuel Hill, the New
Salem merchant. Born April 6, 1831, she
was three or four years old when Lincoln
named her. Mrs. Shipp was the mother
of Laura, the wife of Thomas P. Reep,
the author of this book, and the great-
grandmother of this book's editor,
Constance Reep Unsworth.

that milk?" She was just a young girl lately married, and his calling her Mother embarrassed her; but Lincoln slyly smiled and in his friendly way kept the conversation on safe topics in such a way as to greatly relieve her embarrassment.

Shortly after becoming sole owner, Berry sold the store to the Trent brothers, taking their promissory notes. About the time these came due, the brothers paid them by slipping away while others were sleeping. One morning in the late fall of 1833 the village awoke. Smoke spirals arose from the chimneys, but none arose from the Trent brothers store. Its absence and the closed door attracted the attention of the inhabitants of the village. An examination was made, and no one was seen about the building. Further investigation showed that the Trents had disappeared with their household goods during the night, leaving their creditors holding the bag.

This method of paying debts was common in those days and did not excite the inhabitants, provided the remnants of goods on hand were left.

Lincoln Becomes Responsible for Debts

Not long afterwards, Berry, who had strayed away from the straight and narrow path pointed out to him by his minister father, and who had followed in the footsteps of the prodigal of old, died as a result of his too free access to the flowing bowl, leaving Lincoln to shoulder the burden of all their debts. One ray of sunshine shone through the gloom enveloping Lincoln: James Rutledge insisted upon keeping his agreement with Lincoln to accept Berry's note for Lincoln's debt to him, as before stated.

Other creditors were not so lenient, and when the tally was made, Lincoln was loaded down with debt, which he did not fully pay until 1848, and which he called "the National Debt." One creditor into whose hands one of the Berry & Lincoln notes had fallen, Van Bergen by name, brought suit and, on execution, sold Lincoln's surveying instruments and the horse he rode on his surveying trips, which he had purchased from Thomas Watkins.

Lincoln's good angel, in the person of "Uncle Jimmy" Short, who lived a few miles north of New Salem and who "liked Abe Lincoln," appeared on the scene, bid on the property for $120 and turned it back to Lincoln, who thanked him and said, "Uncle Jimmy, I will do as much for you sometime."

Those words were prophetic. In later years, Short lost his property, and having moved to California to regain his fortune and meeting with little success, he received from President Lincoln, without solicitation upon his part, a commission appointing him Indian Agent. How significant is this act of Lincoln's when compared with those of the average man, who is so prone to forget in his days of prosperity favors done him in his days of adversity.

Lincoln's faculty for making friends who were ready to go the limit for him when occasion demanded was due solely to his own simple, childlike and sincere nature, and his uncompromising fairness and courageous honesty. There was no camouflage about him, no self-conscious dignity.

Skilled with Marbles

As a boy Lincoln had become proficient at marble playing and quoits and never forgot his skill. When as a harbinger of spring the boys of New Salem got out their marbles and began to play, Lincoln, on his walks or during leisure moments in the store, would join them. His skill was such that, if local tradition can be trusted, he could "plump from taw" and knock "old boler" four times out of five. Then in succession he would knock out the four on the corners. And there was no one about New Salem who could beat him pitching quoits, which was then practiced by pitching flat stones. The boys used to take great delight in chasing marbles for him and in praising his skill.

It is said by some writers that, during his presidency, he proceeded one day from the White House to army head-quarters in company with one Wilson, a clerk in the telegraph office, and one of his younger sons. Mr. Lincoln was dressed in a faded linen duster which hung loosely about his angular body. When they got to the street, he reached down and picked up a smooth, round pebble and sent it spinning off his thumb, chal-lenging Wilson and the boy to a game of "follow up."

Each in turn tried to hit the stone farthest in advance, and the game was not won until they reached the steps of the war department. The game was hotly contested, but President Lincoln was finally declared the victor.

Lincoln and the "Underdog"

As illustrative of his thoughtfulness of others and of his kindliness, it is told of him that on a cold day in winter he was walking along Main Street in New Salem and saw a boy by name of Ab Trent chopping at a pile of logs from an old stable that had been pulled down. The wood was hard and dry, and it was hard work for the boy.

James Short. Because he liked
Lincoln, James "Uncle Jimmy" Short
purchased Lincoln's surveying instruments and horse at an auction
held to recover a debt Lincoln owed
to Peter Van Bergen and gave them
back to Lincoln. Years later, Lincoln
repaid the favor when Mr. Short fell
on hard times by appointing him an
Indian Agent in California.

Pausing, Lincoln asked the boy what he was to get for the job, and the boy replied he was to have one dollar. Lincoln then asked him what he was going to do with the dollar when he had earned it, and pointing to his feet which were wrapped in rags, Ab replied, "Buy me a pair of shoes." Lincoln then took the ax and told the boy to run into the store and get warm. Then bending his great strength and skill to the job, Lincoln soon had it finished. He called the boy, handed him the ax, and told him to go collect his dollar and get his shoes.

As is usual with a boy to whom a kindly act is done, Ab was very grateful and became Lincoln's firm friend. He was a very strong Democrat, but at his first opportunity he had determined to disregard party lines and vote for Lincoln. He announced his intention to his friends. In this he was at fault, for as he afterward told Lincoln with tears in his eyes, these friends got him drunk on election day, and to his great sorrow and shame, caused him to vote against Lincoln.

Another incident illustrating Lincoln's sympathy for the "under dog," and his innate kindliness of heart, was his exchanging horses with Dr. Charles Chandler so that the doctor could save his homestead. In 1830, Dr. Chandler had settled near what is now Chandlerville in Cass County. He selected a tract of land and near its center built a cabin and a small stable for his two riding horses. Then he began a widely scattered and poorly paid practice of medicine.

The doctor was so busy and also so in need of his meager earnings to improve and stock his farm that he had neglected to secure title to the land from the government. He felt safe enough however, because there was a code of honor among the settlers, stronger than any written law, that a squatters claim should be held inviolate. But a stranger from

the east by the name of English, who represented a Philadel-
phia capitalist and was out to secure for his principal any choice
tracts of land he could find, came into the neighborhood. Dr.
Chandler met him and lent his assistance in the selection of a
number of desirable tracts, even going so far as to offer one selected for himself.

On his last day in the vicinity, English took dinner with
Dr. Chandler and advised that he was leaving that evening for
Springfield and expected to look over a number of claims on
his way there, and he exhibited a map showing the land he had
selected. Late that afternoon, a settler who lived some ten miles
away on the road to Springfield rode up to Dr. Chandler's
house. The doctor was away calling on some patients, so the
man waited, and when the doctor came home about dusk, the
man hurriedly advised him that the stranger intended to file on
the doctor's claims, and had let the cat out of the bag in a conversation with him that evening.

At that time, land cost two dollars per acre and had to
be paid for with gold or silver coin. Dr. Chandler, not having
sufficient coin for the purpose, set out to find some neighbor
who could and would help him out. After several disappointments, he finally secured the needed funds. Hurrying to his
home, he bestrode his spare horse, and at about midnight, he
started on his ride of forty miles to Springfield.

In the morning between New Salem and Springfield, he
found himself still about twelve miles from his goal, with his
horse exhausted from the grueling trip across country. He was
overtaken by a young man riding a spirited horse. Noting the
condition of the horse the doctor was leading (he had dismounted and was walking to rest the horse) and that the
journey was an urgent one, the young man reined up and in-

Dr. Charles Chandler. Dr. Chandler's homestead was saved from a "land shark" by Lincoln. Lincoln loaned him his fresh horse, replacing the exhausted horse Dr. Chandler was leading, while the doctor was trying to reach the land claim office ahead of a stranger. The stranger, by the name of English, was attempting to register a claim on Dr. Chandler's land before he did.

quired the cause. This was explained by the doctor in a few words, and the young man, without a word, leaped from his horse, shortened the stirrups to fit the doctor's shorter limbs, transferred the saddle bags from the doctor's horse to his own, and said: "There, doctor, mount my horse and leave me yours and don't let any grass grow under his feet on the way. Leave him at Herndon's stables where I will have yours sometime to-day, and we will swap back. I want to get you and your pill bags and the specie into the land office ahead of that shark. No thanks—just go!"

The doctor did as he was bid and, arriving at the land office an hour before English, secured title to his land. The young man who made this possible was Abraham Lincoln. Late that day, he walked into Herndon's stable leading the doctor's horse in much better condition than when he had received him.

Later, Dr. Chandler claimed another 40 acres and, de-termining to have his land surveyed, made inquiries at Spring-field for a surveyor to do the work. Being advised that Cal-houn's deputy lived back at New Salem, he sent word to him to come and survey this land. Imagine the doctor's surprise when, upon Lincoln's arrival, he recognized in the surveyor the young man whose kindly act had saved his homestead for him. Need-less to say, in Dr. Chandler, Lincoln had a real friend, and this friendship continued steadfast during all their later lives.

12 *Lincoln a Candidate Again*

In the spring of 1834, Lincoln again announced his candidacy for the legislature and started his canvass. By this time his acquaintance had spread over the greater part of Sangamon County. Having mastered *Blackstone's Commentaries* through the encouragement of his friend of Black Hawk War days, Major John Stuart, of Springfield, who was also a candidate on the same ticket with Lincoln, he had taken up the study of law systematically, using Stuart's books.

At a later date, in describing his early struggles in learning the law, Lincoln said that on his trips from Springfield to New Salem, sometimes on horseback, at other times on foot, he would frequently read and master as much as 40 pages. On his surveying trips and speech-making tours, he would carry a law book with him and study as he rode along.

Early in his life in New Salem, Lincoln had acquired the habit of carrying with him whatever book he might be studying at the time. He would read as he walked along the streets, then closing the book, his lips would be seen moving as he repeated to himself in his own words the thought he had just read. Meeting friends or acquaintances, he would stop and converse with them, closing the book but marking the place by a finger between the pages. Then passing on, he would again open his book and proceed as before. He was a living example of the application of the couplet from the old schoolbook poem, which school boys were wont to recite years ago:

Take that book from off the shelf,
God helps him who helps himself.

On one occasion, Lincoln went to do work for Russell B. Godbey. At the close of his labor for the day, Lincoln mounted the woodpile, and in his shirt sleeves, with his bare feet hanging down, stretched himself out with a book before his eyes. Godbey, who chanced to pass, asked what he was reading. Lincoln replied he "was not reading, he was studying." Godbey then asked what he was studying, and Lincoln replied, "Law!" The incongruousness of the situation was too much for Godbey, who exclaimed, "Good God Almighty!" and walked on.

Lincoln's Second Campaign

In the 1834 campaign for the legislature, Lincoln rode about the country meeting the people and soliciting their support. When stopping anywhere, he immediately made friends with the children, and gathering the smaller ones upon his knees and with the others about him, he would entertain them while the busy mother prepared the meal.

He would carry in water, and if need be, split wood

with which to cook the meal. If the men folk were engaged in mowing grain, splitting rails, or putting up hay, he would rest them by taking the scythe and mowing a swath, by splitting a few rails, or by pitching hay. Whatever they were engaged in doing, he could and did do as well as or better than they, his great strength and seasoned muscles standing him in good stead. In this manner he made friends wherever he went, and with his good humored jokes and stories, interested and entertained them.

But Lincoln's versatility did not end here. Upon all the live questions of the day and particularly those matters of special interest to his electorate, he talked with convincing eloquence and logic.

It is said that Dr. Barrett, a man of parts and a staunch Whig, upbraiding Lincoln during this canvass, said to one of his friends, "Can't the party raise any better material than that?" After hearing Lincoln's speech, however, the doctor was filled with amazement, and declared, "Lincoln knows more than all the other candidates put together." The election took place the first part of August, and of the four candidates elected, Lincoln received next to the highest number of votes.

13 *Lincoln at Vandalia*

In the December following his election, Lincoln prepared to go to Vandalia, which was then the capital of Illinois,
to attend the session of the legislature. However, he was without funds to purchase suitable clothes, to take care of a few
pressing debts, and to cover the expenses of his trip. He needed
$200.

Coleman Smoot, who was a wealthy farmer and money
lender, came to his rescue and loaned him this sum, which Lincoln repaid with the customary ten percent interest added, "according to promise," as later stated by Mr. Smoot.

Shortly afterwards, dressed in a new suit of butternut
jeans, and taking leave of his sweetheart, Ann Rutledge, he
made his way to Vandalia and took up his duties as a lawmaker.
The assembly at this time was composed of 81 members: 26
senators and 55 representatives. The salary of a representative
was three dollars per day during the time the legislature was in
session.

The state furnished a cork inkstand, a few quills, and a
small amount of stationery to each member. Lincoln did noth-

ing spectacular during this session but seemed content to study his fellow members with a view to comparing himself with them and to correcting his own deficiencies.

Among the legislators he met were Governor Duncan, Jesse K. DuBois, Stephen T. Logan, William L. D. Ewing and others, men who afterwards made their mark upon the history of their state and nation. He also met Stephen A. Douglas, who was making a campaign for District Attorney in his district or circuit, which at that time included the county in which the state capitol was located.

In one respect at least, Lincoln was efficient. He was always in his place, paying strict attention to what was going on. His first official act was to serve notice that he would ask leave to introduce a bill limiting the jurisdiction of justices of the peace, which he succeeded in passing. Outside of a few motions, which it appears were lost from the journal of that session, this was all that was done by Lincoln during that term; but he had made many friends and was known as an adept storyteller.

Lincoln Returns to New Salem

In the spring of 1835, Lincoln returned to New Salem and Ann Rutledge, took up his duties of postmaster and surveyor, and resumed the study of law with greater vigor than ever. Ann had spent her year attending school at Jacksonville, and if fortune smiled upon Lincoln, this was to be the year of their marriage.

The Rutledge family had removed to a farm a few miles north of New Salem, and Lincoln had a great deal of business in that vicinity. Ann had frequent occasion to visit New Salem,

and at such times met Lincoln, except when he was away surveying. The Rutledge family was friendly to his suit, and David, Ann's older brother, was Lincoln's friend and associate.

Mary Ann (Miller) Rutledge. Wife of
James Rutledge and mother of Ann
Rutledge, she was born in Kentucky
on October 21, 1787. She married
James Rutledge in Kentucky on
January 25, 1808, and died in Iowa
on December 26, 1878. She was
hostess at the New Salem Inn from
1829 to 1833 or 1834. She then
moved with her husband and family
to a farm, where her daughter Ann
died August 25, 1835. Her husband
James died later the same year.

14 *Ann Rutledge's Death*

The world was bright and pleasant to Abe Lincoln and Ann Rutledge, and every passing day brought the time for the consummation of their love nearer. Then Ann learned that her old lover, McNamar, was still alive, that he was not what she had thought him to be, and, with his mother and sisters, was coming back to New Salem.

Troubled by pangs of conscience, and given to self-analysis in which she blamed herself for her own lack of faithfulness to her vows of first love, she felt that she would justly merit any denunciation and reproach that he might heap upon her. But she also felt that she could not give up the new love that had come into her life. She soon worried herself into such a condition, physically, as to become an easy prey to the fevers prevalent at that time. So she sickened and was soon confined to her bed. The best physicians in the vicinity were called in but failed to check the ravages of the fever.

She asked for Lincoln, and he was sent for. After admitting him to the sick room, those present retired, leaving them alone together. What was said by them at this last leave-

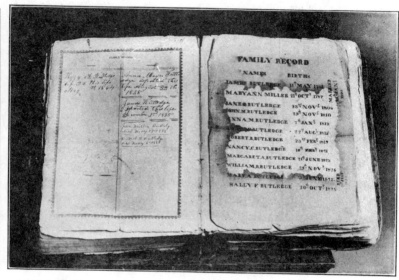

The old Rutledge Family Bible. The Bible was published in 1814. The date of Ann Rutledge's death was handwritten in it by her father. The Bible was donated to the Old Salem Lincoln League by Sarah (Rutledge) Saunders, Ann Rutledge's youngest sister. Mrs. Saunders, in her statement accompanying the gift, said "I heard my mother often say, 'I have seen Lincoln read from this book more than once.'"

taking, none knew but she and Lincoln, and so far as is known, he never told. It is only known that when he left the room, his shoulders were bowed with grief, and the tears were streaming down his cheeks.

Shortly afterward, Ann Rutledge died. She was buried in the little graveyard near the Rutledge home at Concord. Lincoln was disconsolate. From her funeral he returned grief-stricken to New Salem.

Deserting the haunts of men, he wandered over the hills and through the woods and by the banks of the river. He did not eat. Sleep was unknown to him. His friends became alarmed at his conduct.

Bowling Green Took Lincoln Home

Fearing for Lincoln's reason, Bowling Green found him, took him to his home, gave him a room, and looked after him. Aunt Nancy, Green's wife, mothered him and carried him sympathy and food until the poignancy of his grief was assuaged and he came to be himself again. His was too strong a character to give up wholly to despair, and as time passed, he became his old self once more; yet his life thereafter was somehow different.

Times would come when Lincoln's mind would go back to his early love, and his sorrow would be revived. He made many pilgrimages to the little graveyard at Concord that contained Ann's mortal remains. He would sit by the side of her grave, seeking to commune with her in spirit. To his more intimate friends, he said, "My heart is buried there with Ann Rutledge." On a blustery, rainy, windy night, when Lincoln was visiting his friend William G. Greene, the pattering of the rain

This was the old home of Bowling Green, located at the
foot of the bluffs about a half mile north of New Salem,
as it appeared about 1918. It was in an upper room of
this building that Lincoln stayed following the death of
Ann Rutledge. He stayed here at various intervals from
1831 to 1837.

upon the roof, the soughing of the wind through the trees, and the flash of the lightning so affected him that, with the tears streaming down his face, he bowed his head upon his breast and sobbed aloud.

When questioned by Greene as to the cause of his grief and asked to control himself, he replied, "I cannot, Bill, I cannot. I am overcome with grief when I think of the storm, and of the rain beating on her grave."

Long years after, Lincoln, in speaking of Ann Rutledge to a friend, is reported to have said, "I truly loved the girl." After hesitating a moment, he added, "and I have loved the name of Rutledge ever since."

It was during this period that Lincoln's religious beliefs changed. At first, his overwhelming grief at the loss of his loved one made him bitter and reinforced his doubts as to the divinity of Jesus Christ and the presence everywhere of an all wise and merciful God. But Dr. Allen, a sincere Christian, as efficient in the cure of the souls as of the bodies of his patients, called often on Lincoln at the Bowling Green home, and with his heart full of sympathy for his suffering friend, and with wise patience, he gained Lincoln's confidence and helped him to better understand the "Eternal verities of God."

In time, the seeds sown by Dr. Allen in Lincoln's fertile mind led him back to the simple faith of his mother and the trust and confidence in his Maker that was possessed by his departed love.

Dr. John Allen. Dr. Allen treated Lincoln
following Ann Rutledge's death. Besides
restoring Lincoln's physical health, he
helped to restore Lincoln's confidence in
his mother's Christian faith and his interest in life. Dr. Allen organized the
first Temperance Society in New Salem.
As a conscientious Christian, he treated
patients on Sunday, but donated the
money earned to worthy causes. Dr.
Allen moved to Petersburg, Illinois
about 1839 where he later died.

15 *Lincoln Loses His First Case*

From this time on, Lincoln made his home for a considerable portion of the time with his friend, Bowling Green. It was here upon a Sunday morning, while stretched out upon the cellar door reading law, that he, for the first time, met Richard Yates, who during Lincoln's presidency was war governor of Illinois. Yates had come up from Jacksonville to spend the weekend with his friend William G. Greene and was taken by Greene to New Salem to meet his friend, Abe Lincoln.

From that beginning there grew up a close and firm friendship between the two that endured for life. Lincoln continued to pursue his study of the law when not employed at surveying, and he began to take an interest in the trials in the justice's courts.

Long before this time, Lincoln had learned to write simple contracts, deeds and mortgages. While surveying in the vicinity of Concord, he learned through Robert Clary and David M. Rutledge, who were carrying the news, that there was a hearing that afternoon in a bastardy suit before Squire Samuel Berry. The defendant had employed Berry's brother-in-law, who was visiting him and claimed to have been licensed to practice law, to look after his interests. The girl, who was very poor, had no lawyer.

Lincoln's love of fair play caused him to suspend his surveying and to offer his services to the girl, which she thankfully accepted. Most of the witnesses were timid old ladies not accustomed to court proceedings, but they were Lincoln's friends. During the examination of these witnesses, he succeeded in putting them at their ease by calling them by their given names, Aunt Polly and Aunt Sally, and in his friendly, easy way, guiding them in their testimony.

In his address to the court at the close of the evidence, Lincoln likened a *man's* character in a case like this to a piece of white cloth, which, though it became soiled, yet could be washed and hung out in the sun, and by the aid of the water, sun and air, would become white again. But that the character of the *girl*, who was no more to blame, and in most instances not nearly so much to blame as the man, was like a broken and shattered bottle or glass vessel, which could not be restored or made whole again.

Lincoln's First Case

Probably the first suit in a court of justice in which Lincoln appeared as counsel was that of the Trent brothers against Jack Kelso to recover possession of a hog. It took place shortly after the Trents had purchased the Berry & Lincoln store. Hogs were not kept penned up in those days but were allowed to roam about at will and root for their subsistence. Lincoln, appearing for the Trent brothers, proved by three witnesses that the hog belonged to them. Kelso testified that the hog belonged to him, but he was unsupported by witnesses.

After Kelso finished his testimony, Squire Bowling Green, before whom the case was tried, asked if there were any further witnesses. Being advised to the contrary, he announced his judgment in favor of the defendant, Kelso. Lincoln was astonished and lingered behind after the litigants had left. He then called the attention of the court to the rule of evidence, which required a case of fact to be determined in accordance with the greater weight or preponderance of the testimony. Green replied, "Abe, the first duty of a court is to decide cases justly and in accordance with the truth. I know that shoat myself, and I know it belongs Kelso and that the plaintiffs and their witnesses lied."

It is said that Lincoln did not charge any fees in the trial of cases before justices because he had not been admitted to practice law. And while he wrote many deeds, mortgages, and simple contracts for his friends in and about New Salem, he rarely received or charged for them.

Mary Owens

Among Lincoln's intimate friends were Dr. Bennett Able and his wife, who lived near New Salem. Mrs. Able's maiden name was Owens, and she hailed from the state of Kentucky. A sister, Mary, had visited Mrs. Able a year or two before, and Lincoln had met her.

A year after Ann Rutledge's death, Lincoln had occasion to deliver a letter to Mrs. Able. She told him the letter was from her sister Mary, and that she was shortly to go to Kentucky for a visit and was going to bring Mary back with her with the hope and expectation that Lincoln would become her brother-in-law. She said that he had reached the age and time of life when he needed a wife to make a home for him. Lincoln, falling in with her suggestion, stated that if she would do this and he did not become her brother-in-law, it would be through no fault of his. In due time the trip was made, and Mrs. Able returned, her sister accompanying her.

True to his word, Lincoln called upon the young lady. Instead of the slender, blooming maiden of his former acquaintance, he found a mature woman with an over-abundance of adipose tissue and with teeth indicating an excessive use of sweets. But swallowing his disappointment, he gallantly pressed his suit, but he did not bring the matter finally to an issue until after his removal to Springfield in 1837, when he wrote the following letters, which show the exact state of his feelings better than any words of ours.

Friend Mary,

You will no doubt think it rather strange that I should write you a letter on the same day on which we parted; and I can only account for it by supposing that seeing you lately makes me think of you more than usual, while at our late meeting, we had but few expressions of thoughts. You must know that I cannot see you or think of you with entire indifference; and yet it may be that you are mistaken in regard to what my real feelings toward you are. If I knew you were not, I should not trouble you with this letter. Perhaps any other man would know enough without further information, but I consider it my peculiar right to plead ignorance and your bounden duty to allow the plea.

I want in all cases to do right; and most particularly so in all cases with women. I want, at this particular time, more than anything else, to do right with you, and if I knew it would be doing right, as I rather suspect it would, to let you alone, I would do it. And for the purpose of making the matter as plain as possible, I now say, that you can now drop the subject, dismiss your thoughts (if you ever had any) from me forever, and leave this letter unanswered, without calling forth one accusing murmur from me. And I will even go further, and say, that if it will add anything to your comfort or peace of mind to do so, it is my sincere wish that you should. Do not understand by this that I wish to cut your acquaintance. I mean no such thing. What I do wish is that our further acquaintance shall depend upon yourself. If such further acquaintance would contribute nothing to your happiness, I am sure it would not to mine. If you feel yourself in any degree bound to me, I am now willing to release you, provided you wish it; while, on the other hand, I am willing and even anxious to bind you faster if I can be convinced that it will in any considerable degree add to your happiness. This, indeed, is the whole question with me. Nothing would make me more miserable, nothing more happy, than to know you were so.

In what I have now said, I think I cannot be misunderstood; and to make myself understood is the sole object of this....

If it suits you best to not answer this--farewell--a long life and a merry one attend you. But if you conclude to write back, speak as plainly as I do. There can be neither harm nor danger in saying to me anything you think, just in the manner you think it.

My respects to your sister.
Your friend, Lincoln.

The following letter to Mrs. Browning no doubt was intended for no eyes but hers and her husband's, being much more frank than it otherwise would have been.

Springfield,
April 1, 1838

Dear Madam:—

Without apologizing for being so egotistical, I shall make the history of so much of my life as has elapsed since I saw you the subject of this letter. And, by the way, I now discover that, in order to give a full and intelligent account of the things I have done and suffered since I saw you, I shall necessarily have to relate some that happened before.

It was, then, in the autumn of 1836 that a married lady of my acquaintance and who was a great friend of mine, being about to pay a visit to her father and other relatives residing in Kentucky, proposed to me that on her return she would bring a sister of hers with her on condition that I would engage to become her brother-in-law with all convenient dispatch. I, of course, accepted the proposal, for you know I could not have done otherwise, had I really been averse to it; but privately, between you and me, I was most confoundedly well pleased with the project. I had seen the said sister some three years before, thought her intelligent and agreeable, and saw no good objection to plodding life through hand in hand with her. Time passed on, the lady took her journey, and in due time returned, sister in company sure enough. This stomached me a little; for it appeared to me that her coming so readily showed that she was a trifle too willing; but, on reflection, it occurred to me that she might have been prevailed on by her married sister to come, without anything concerning me ever having been mentioned to her; and so I concluded that, if no other objection presented itself, I would consent to waive this. All this occurred to me on hearing of her arrival in the neighborhood; for, be it remembered, I had not yet seen her, except about all things to stick to my word, especially if others had been induced to three years previous, as above mentioned. In a few days we had an interview; and, although I had seen her before, she did not look as my imagination had pictured her. I knew she was over-size, but she now appeared a fair match for Falstaff. I knew she was called an 'old maid,' and I felt no doubt of the truth of at least half of the appellation; but now, when I beheld her, I could not for my life avoid thinking of my mother; and this, not from withered features, for her skin was too full of fat to permit of its contracting into wrinkles, but from her want of teeth, weather-beaten appearance in general, and from a kind of notion that ran in my head that nothing could have commenced at the size of infancy and reached her present bulk in less than thirty-five or forty years; and, in short, I was not at all pleased with her. But what could I do? I had told her sister I would take her for better or for worse; and I made a point of honor and conscience in act on it, which in this case I had no doubt they had; for I was now fairly convinced that no other man on earth would have her, and hence the conclusion that they were bent on holding me to my bargain. 'Well,' thought I, 'I have said it, and, be the consequences what they may, it shall not be my fault if I fail to do it.' At once I determined to consider her my wife; and, this done, all my powers of discovery were put to work in search of perfections in her which might be fairly set off against her defects. I tried to imagine her handsome, which, but for her unfortunate corpulency, was actually true. Exclusive of this, no woman that I have ever seen has a finer face. I also tried to convince myself that the mind was much more to be valued than the person; and in this she was not inferior, as I could discover, to any with whom I had been acquainted.

Shortly after this, without coming to any positive understanding with her, I set out for Vandalia, where and when you first saw me. During my stay there I had letters from her which did not change my opinion of either lie, intellect or intention, but on the contrary confirmed it in both.

All this while, although I was fixed, 'firm as the surge-repelling rock,' in my resolution, I found I was continually resenting the rashness which had led me to make it. Through life, I have been in no bondage, either real or imaginary, from the thralldom of which I so much desired to be free. After my return home, I saw nothing to change my opinion of her in any particular. She was the same, and so was I. I now spent my time in planning how I might get along through life after my contemplated change of circumstances should have taken place, and how I might procrastinate the evil day for a time, which I really dreaded as much, perhaps more, than an Irishman does the halter.

After all my suffering upon this deeply interesting subject, here I am, wholly, unexpectedly, completely, out of the 'scrape,' and now I want to know if you can guess how I got out of it—out, clear, in every sense of the term; no violation of word, honor, or conscience. I don't believe you can guess, and so I might as well tell you at once. As the lawyer says, it was done in the manner following, to-wit: After I had delayed the matter so long as I thought I could in honor do (which, by the way, had brought me round into the last fall), I concluded I might as well bring it to a consummation without further delay; and so I mustered my resolution, and made the proposal to her direct; but, shocking to relate, she answered 'No.' At first I supposed she did it through an affectation of modesty, which I thought but ill became her under the peculiar circumstances of her case; but on my renewal of the charge, I found she repelled it with greater firmness than before. I tried it again and again, but with the same success, or rather with the same want of success.

I was finally forced to give it up; at which I very unexpectedly found myself mortified almost beyond endurance. I was mortified, it seemed to me, in a hundred different ways. My vanity was deeply wounded by the reflection that I had been too stupid to discover her intentions, and at the same time never doubting that I understood them perfectly; and also that she, whom I had taught myself to believe nobody else would have, had actually rejected me with all my fancied greatness. And, to cap the whole, I then for the first time began to suspect that I was really a little in love with her. But let it all go. I'll try and outlive it. Others have been made fools of by the girls; but this can never with truth be said of me. I most emphatically, in this instance, made a fool of myself. I have now come to the conclusion never again to think of marrying, and for this reason: I can never be satisfied with anyone who would be blockhead enough to have me.

When you receive this, write me, a long yarn about something to amuse me. Give my respects to Mr. Browning.

Your sincere friend,
A. Lincoln.

16 *Lincoln Runs for the Third Time*

In the spring of 1836, Lincoln decided to make the race for the legislature again. This time he had a much wider acquaintance and the prestige of having served one term. If he had done nothing startling in the way of securing new legislation or to excite the interest or attention of the state at large, neither had he been guilty of any act of indiscretion that in any way affected his popularity with his constituents.

So when he entered upon this third campaign for election to the legislature, his popularity was greater than ever. During the preceding term, the legislature had increased the number of its representatives in Sangamon County to seven and its senators to two, making nine in all. There being no nominating convention in which to nominate candidates for the respective political parties, the right to be a candidate for election was open to all.

Lincoln again made his announcement by means of a political handbill in which he set out his platform and the things for which he would stand if elected. This platform he published in the *Springfield Journal*, as follows:

New Salem, June 13, 1836.

To the Editor of *The Journal*:

In your paper of last Saturday I see a communication over the signature of "Many Voters" in which the candidates who are announced in *The Journal* are called upon to show their hands. Agreed. Here's mine:

I go for all sharing the privileges of the government who assist in bearing it burdens. Consequently, I go for admitting all whites to the right of suffrage who pay taxes or bear arms (by no means excluding females).

If elected I shall consider the whole people of Sangamon my constituents, as well those that oppose as those that support me.

While acting as their representative, I shall be governed by their will on subjects upon which I have the means of knowing what their will is; and upon others I shall do what my own judgment teaches me will best advance their interest. Whether elected or not, I go for distributing the proceeds of the sales of public lands to the several States to enable our State, in common with others, to dig canals and construct railroads without borrowing money and paying the interest on it.

If alive on the first Monday in November, I shall vote for Hugh L. White, for President.

Very respectfully,

A. Lincoln.

That Lincoln was far ahead of his time is evidenced by the concluding sentence of the second paragraph in which he expresses himself as in favor of women's suffrage. If the principle is right now, it was right then.

As stated by William H. Herndon in his *Life of Lincoln*, Lincoln had pronounced views with reference to the great questions of moral and social reforms, under which he classed universal suffrage, temperance, and slavery. "All such questions," he observed one day as they were discussing temperance in the office, "must find lodgment with the most enlightened souls who stamp them with their approval. In God's own time they will be organized into law and thus woven into the fabric of our institutions."

In this canvass there were many joint discussions between the opposing candidates, in all of which Lincoln took a prominent part. Following the practice of the time, Lincoln was usually accompanied by a number of his friends from New Salem who would take up their positions in different parts of the audience to lead the applause and to hector the opposing candidate.

The "Skewed Line"

Another incident that illustrates Lincoln's kindly disposition and serves to explain why men followed him and loved to serve him is that of the "skewed line" in Petersburg.

When he was called upon to survey the original town of Petersburg in February, 1836, he found that Jemima Elmore, the widow of an old friend who had been a member of his company in the Black Hawk War, had bought a little tract of land within the grounds to be surveyed and had built a home where she lived with her children. If the streets of Petersburg were to run straight north and south, a part of her house would be in the street.

To save the house, he set his compass to run south one degree east, and ran the cross streets at right angles to the north and south streets. One result of this "skewing" of the lines was that there was an irregular strip left on both the north and south side of the town, the strip on the south being 37½ feet wide at the west end and 84½ feet wide at the east end.

Scandal Insinuated

During the absence of Lincoln, Colonel Robert Allen, who was a brother of Dr. John Allen of New Salem and of considerable local prominence as a Democratic politician, visited New Salem and insinuated that he knew certain facts which, if known to the public, would damn both Lincoln and Ninnian W. Edwards—a candidate on the same ticket—but that he purposed to keep his knowledge to himself out of personal consideration for Lincoln.

Naturally, this statement of the Colonel's aroused the curiosity of Lincoln's New Salem friends, and since there was nothing in his life or conduct that the public did not nor might not know, Lincoln immediately called Colonel Allen's hand, as shown in the following letter:

New Salem, June 21, 1836.

Dear Colonel:

I am told that during my absence last week you passed

through the place and stated publicly that you were in possession of facts which if known to the public would entirely destroy the prospects of N. W. Edwards and myself at the ensuing election, but that through favor to us you would forbear to divulge them. No one has needed favors more than I, and generally few have been less unwilling to accept them, but in this case, favor to me would be injustice to the public, and therefore I must beg your pardon for declining it. That I once had the confidence of the people of Sangamon County is sufficiently evident; and if I have done anything, either by design or misadventure, which if known, would subject me to a forfeiture of that confidence, he that knows of that thing, and conceals it, is a traitor to his country's interest.

I find myself wholly unable to form any conjecture of what fact or facts, real or supposed, you spoke; but my opinion of your veracity will not permit me for a moment to doubt that you at least believed what you said. I am flattered with the personal regard you manifested for me; but I do hope that on mature reflection you will view the public interest as a paramount consideration and therefore let the worst come.

I assure you that the candid statement of facts on your part, however low it may sink me, shall never break the ties of personal friendship between us.

I wish an answer to this, and you are at liberty to publish both if you choose.

Very respectfully,

A. Lincoln.

Colonel Allen failed to make known his "facts" or to reply to this letter. He appears to have sought the tall timber and to have remained in seclusion during the remainder of the campaign.

It was during this campaign that Lincoln exhibited those peculiar qualities of mind and heart that later were to endear him to the great mass of people. In a speech following that of his friend and colleague Ninnian Edwards, who was a man of quick and fiery temper and who had retorted in a very angry manner to the aspersions of an opponent, arousing the different factions to fighting heat, Lincoln poured oil upon the troubled waters. First quieting his auditors, Lincoln launched into one of the most eloquent and convincing speeches he had ever made, carrying the crowd with him almost to a man.

Lincoln Has To Be "Taken Down"

When the crowd was about to disperse, one George Forquer, fearing the political effect of Lincoln's speech, asked to be heard. Forquer was a man of mature years and of recognized ability as a lawyer and politician who had recently left the Whigs and joined the Democratic party, immediately following which he had been appointed register of the land office at a salary of $3,000 per year and who possessed the only lightning rod in Springfield. He began his speech by saying that the young man who had just spoken would have to be taken down and that he was sorry the task had fallen upon him.

In his attitude throughout his speech, Forquer assumed an air of superiority and veiled contempt for the awkward and ungainly youth, which stirred up Lincoln's resentment. Listening intently, his face expressing suppressed excitement, Lincoln immediately following the close of Forquer's address, stepped upon the platform to make reply.

As said by Mr. Herndon, in quoting Joshua Speed, who was present on this occasion, "I have heard him often since in the courts and before the people, but never saw him appear and acquit himself as well as upon that occasion.

"His reply to Forquer was characterized by great dignity and force. I shall never forget the conclusion of that speech: 'Mr. Forquer commenced his speech by announcing that the young man would have to be taken down. It is for you, fellow citizens, not for me to say whether I am up, or down. The gentleman has seen fit to allude to my being a young man; but he forgets that I am older in years than I am in the tricks and trades of politicians. I desire to live, and I desire place and distinction; but I would rather die now than, like the gentleman, live to see the day that I would change my politics for an office worth $3,000 a year, and then feel compelled to erect a lightning rod to protect a guilty conscience from an offended God.' The effect of this rejoinder was wonderful and gave Forquer and his lightning rod a notoriety, the extent of which none envied him."

William Henry Herndon was a law partner and biographer of Lincoln's, and "...had a ...better understanding of his complex personality than any other student ever had," according to David Herbert Donald at Harvard University. "For this reason, for all its limitations, Herndon's *Life of Lincoln* remains a classic—the essential book that any serious student of Abraham Lincoln must read," added Donald. First published in 1889, Herndon's biography of Lincoln is still available from Da Capo Press, and is now titled, *Herndon's Life of Lincoln.* Rowan Herndon, who sold his half of the Herndon brothers' store in New Salem to Lincoln, creating the Berry & Lincoln store, was a cousin of William Henry Herndon.

17 *Election of the "Long Nine"*

At the ensuing election, the whole Whig ticket was elected, with Abraham Lincoln receiving the largest number of votes of any of the nine Sangamon County candidates. Those candidates were all large men, averaging over six feet in height and over two hundred pounds in weight, and as this was the largest delegation from any one district and they all worked together, they soon came to be known as the "long nine."

This session was one of the most important that had ever been held in the State of Illinois. Much money was spent in the way of public improvements, and however much the wisdom of this at that time might be questioned, Lincoln only represented his constituents and party in this, and they showed their approval by electing him to succeed himself in the two following elections.

William Henry Herndon, who was Lincoln's law partner for a number of years, says of him, "He never had what some people call 'money sense.' By reason of his peculiar nature and construction, he was endowed with none of the elements of a political economist. He was enthusiastic and theoretical to a certain degree; and could take hold of, and wrap himself up in, a great moral question; but in dealing with the financial and commercial interests of a community or government, he was equally as inadequate as he was ineffectual in managing the economy of his own household."

From Vandalia to Springfield

The matter most important to Lincoln's constituents that was done by this legislature was the removal of the state capital from Vandalia to Springfield. The management of the bill for this purpose was entrusted to Lincoln. The fight was a warm one. Twice it was laid upon the table by its opponents. In the darkest moments, Lincoln never despaired of ultimate success. By his shrewd knowledge of human nature and wise counsels, he rallied his forces and won the day, securing the passage of the bill by both houses a day or two before the close of the session.

Slavery Question Comes Up

The slavery question was beginning to agitate the minds of the people. In a legislature, most of whose members were from the South, it would not be expected that there would be anything but pro-slavery sentiment. Such was the case in this legislature when a resolution was introduced disapproving the formation of abolition societies and of the doctrine promulgated by them, and setting out that "the right of property in slaves is secured to the slaveholding states by the federal constitution, and that they cannot be deprived of that right without their consent."

"That the general government cannot abolish slavery in the District of Columbia against the consent of the citizens of said district, without a manifest breach of good faith."

Lincoln was opposed to its passage and solicited his colleagues to join him in signing a carefully worded protest against the same. This they all declined to do, except one, Dan Stone. The protest was prepared by Lincoln and so carefully worded that his position in opposition to slavery was maintained without any commitment as to the manner in which that opposition was to become effective. The protest was in the following words:

Resolutions upon the subject of domestic slavery having passed both branches of the General Assembly at its present session, the undersigned hereby protest against the passage of the same.

They believe that the institution of slavery is founded on both injustice and bad policy, but that the promulgation of abolition doctrines tends rather to increase than abate its evils.

They believe that the congress of the United States has no power under the constitution to interfere with the institution of slavery in the different states.

They believe that the congress of the United States has the power under the constitution to abolish slavery in the District of Columbia, but that the power ought not to be exercised unless at the request of the people of the district.

The difference between these opinions and those contained in the above resolutions is their reason for entering this protest.

DAN STONE,
A. LINCOLN,
Representatives from the county of Sangamon.

The protest declares that he "believes that the institution of slavery is founded on both injustice and bad policy." Lincoln, from the time he expressed his intention, "If I ever get a chance to hit that thing, I'll hit it hard," until his emancipation proclamation destroying slavery in the United States, never swerved from the line he had laid out for himself.

On their return from Vandalia, the "long nine" were met and escorted to Springfield by a triumphal procession. They were welcomed by public dinners and much speech making, and their praises were sung by the local orators and inhabitants, Lincoln receiving the lion's share.

Admitted to Practice Law

Before leaving Springfield for his New Salem home, Lincoln had been licensed to practice law and had consummated plans to enter into partnership with his old friend of Black Hawk War days, Major John T. Stuart, who had been his colleague in the preceding legislature and from whom he had borrowed textbooks on the law.

Major John T. Stuart. Major Stuart
probably had more to do with shap-
ing the political destiny and professional life of Lincoln than anyone.
Lincoln and Major Stuart first met
and became friends during the Black
Hawk War and remained friends
afterwards. Lincoln began his sys-
tematic study of the law under Stuart's direction. He borrowed Stuart's
books, and when admitted to practice in the spring of 1837, formed a
partnership with Stuart. Both men
had the same political beliefs and
were members of the Illinois legislature together. Major Stuart was
elected to Congress twice. He died
in Springfield, Illinois, in 1885.

18 *Lincoln Returns and Visits Ann Rutledge's Grave*

Lincoln then made his way back to New Salem. He made his way back to the scenes of his labors of the preceding six years, where he had come, as he later said, "a strange, friendless, uneducated, penniless boy, working on a flatboat at ten dollars per month," like a piece of floating driftwood upon the current of the placid Sangamon; where he had, by his physical prowess and sheer strength of mind and will, tamed the wild and reckless gang from Clary's Grove and made them his willing followers and staunchest supporters and friends; where, by constant application, he had mastered the elements of English grammar and acquired a sufficient knowledge of the higher mathematics to enable him to do well and accurately all plain surveying; where he had read Shakespeare and Burns and other standard works of poetry and prose and had mastered the law; where he had met and loved, and patiently waited to declare that love, and wooed and won and, by death, lost Ann Rutledge.

Here he had formed the closest and most enduring friendships of his life. The name of Honest Abe, here acquired, followed him throughout his life, and whether at Springfield or at Washington, he was always ready to extend to the friends of New Salem days a helping hand and a hearty welcome to his house and home.

What must have been his thoughts on the long trip from Springfield to New Salem on this sad occasion? What thoughts of his lost love? How saddened he must have been when he considered his removal from the scenes of his long association with her, and from his old friends who had proved their friendship by their acts as well as their words!

At the Grave

Local tradition has it that he stole away to the old Concord cemetery, probably for the last time. There at the grave of Ann Rutledge he sought answers to many of the most perplexing problems of religion and life, and held communion in spirit with her and gained hope and faith and new strength to meet the burdens of his new duties and new ambitions in life.

Then, as quietly as he had come, with few additional worldly effects, but immeasurably richer in experience and life, in education of heart and intellect, in strength of character, in all those qualities that go to the making of a Man, he left New Salem, fully qualified and equipped to take up the duties and responsibilities of the larger life before him.

The grave of Ann Rutledge. Ann Rutledge died August 25, 1835 and was buried at Concord Cemetery, about three or four miles from Petersburg, Illinois. About 60 years later, her body was exhumed and removed from Concord Cemetery by Samuel Montgomery, a Petersburg undertaker. Ann Rutledge was reburied in Oakland Cemetery on the southwest outskirts of Petersburg. The boulder pictured here, with her name as shown, was from New Salem. It was replaced in 1922 with a more imposing monument.

19 New Salem Deserted

Following Lincoln's removal to Springfield, the village of New Salem began to decline. The town of Petersburg, which was more accessible than New Salem, had been surveyed and laid out by Abraham Lincoln in February, 1836.

Early in the year of 1839, Menard County was established by the legislature, being cut off of the north end of Sangamon County. The next step was to establish the county seat, and in a contest between it and New Market, Huron, and Miller's Ferry, Petersburg won. This hurried the downfall of New Salem. One by one the inhabitants left, many of them taking their houses, as well as their goods, with them, until in 1840 only ten houses remained.

Among these was the Rutledge Inn; the Dr. John Allen house, though he had moved to Petersburg and the house was occupied by Henry Traylor; the Rowan Herndon house; the Hill residence and store, then called the Hill Tavern; and the Bale carding-machine house and storeroom for wool. By 1845, only two buildings were left and one of these, the Rutledge Inn, was occupied by Jacob Bale, who had purchased it from

Nelson Alley in 1837. In 1841 he secured a deed to all the unplotted land in the quarter section still belonging to Cameron, together with the Bale lots.

The old Rutledge Inn, to those whose recollections went back only to 1842 or 1843, came to be known as the Jacob Bale house. A drawing was made of this building and a cut of the same was shown in the Atlas Map of Menard County, published in 1874, and is shown on the next page in this book Originally the building had three rooms below and one large room upstairs in which all the men boarders slept. It was a matter of frequent occurrence for the boarders to lie awake till late at night listening to Lincoln tell stories.

RUINS OF
SALEM HOTEL, LINCOLNS BOARDING HOUSE

This is an actual drawing of the Salem Hotel, published in 1874. There are varying accounts of how the building appeared. One account said it was a two story, eight room building. William Henry Herndon had written that it was a "small log building containing four rooms and covered by clapboards." Ida Tarbell said it "…was the first to be built and the last to remain, and that it was a story and a half house, built of logs and containing five rooms." It was owned and occupied by Jacob Bale at the time of his death, years after New Salem disappeared as a town. It was originally the Rutledge Inn.

Judge C. J. F. Clarke. Judge Clarke
was born in New Hampshire on December 10, 1806. He moved to Illinois and settled in New Salem early
in 1833. He boarded at the Rutledge
Inn for a while after his arrival. His
daughter, Lou Clarke, reported that
she heard her father say many times
that the men boarders all slept upstairs together in one large room
and were kept awake until midnight
listening to Lincoln's stories. Judge
Clarke later bought a farm near New
Salem and lived there until he died in
1870.

Stephen A. Douglas, 1813—1861.
Lincoln first met Stephen Douglas in
Vandalia, Illinois, when Lincoln was
elected to the state legislature. At the
time, Douglas was campaigning for the
office of District Attorney in the county
that included Vandalia. Years later,
while campaigning for re-election as an
Illinois Senator in 1858, Senator Douglas was challenged to seven debates
about slavery by Lincoln, his Republican
challenger. Senator Douglas did not un-
derestimate Lincoln: "I shall have my
hands full," Douglas said of Lincoln. "He
is the strong man of his party—full of
wit, facts, dates—the best stump
speaker, with his droll ways, in the
west."

•*Further Reading*•

Catton, Bruce. *The Coming Fury.* New York: Doubleday, 1961.

Dorf, Philip. *Highlights & Sidelights of the Civil War.* Middletown, Connecticut: Southfarm Press, 1989.

Fehrenbacher, Don E. (editor). *Abraham Lincoln: A Documentary Portrait Through His Speeches and Writings.* Stanford: Stanford University Press, 1994.

Good, Timothy S. (editor). *We Saw Lincoln Shot: One Hundred Eyewitness Accounts.* Jackson, Mississippi: University Press of Mississippi, 1995.

Herndon, William Henry. *Herndon's Life of Lincoln: The History and Personal Recollections of Abraham Lincoln.* New York: Da Capo Press, 1983.

Holzer, Harold (editor). *Lincoln as I Knew Him: Gossip, Tributes and Revelations from His Best Friends and Worse Enemies.* Chapel Hill, North Carolina: Algonquin Books, 1999.

Lincoln, Abraham, Fehrenbacher, Virginia (editors), Fehrenbacher, Don. E. *Recollected Words of Abraham Lincoln.* Stanford: Stanford University Press, 1996.

Lincoln, Abraham, Humes, James C. *The Wit & Wisdom of Abraham Lincoln: A Treasury of Quotations, Anecdotes, and Observations.* New York: Gramercy, 1999.

Mitgang, Herbert (editor). *Abraham Lincoln: A Press Portrait.* Athens, Georgia: University of Georgia Press, 1994.

Morris, Jan. *Lincoln: A Foreigner's Quest.* New York: Simon & Schuster, 1999.

Oates, Stephen B. *With Malice Toward None: The Life of Abraham Lincoln.* New York: Harper & Row, 1977.

Old Salem Lincoln League. *Lincoln and New Salem.* Petersburg, Illinois: The Old Salem Lincoln League, 1918.

Old Salem Lincoln League. *Prospectus of the Old Salem Lincoln League for Restoration of New Salem, the Early Home of Abraham Lincoln.* Petersburg, Illinois: The Old Salem Lincoln League, 1918.

Radford, Victoria (editor). *Meeting Mr. Lincoln: Firsthand Recollections of Abraham Lincoln by People, Great and Small, Who Met the President.* Chicago: Ivan R. Dee, Inc., 1998.

Reep, Thomas P. *Lincoln at New Salem.* Petersburg, Illinois: The Old Salem Lincoln League, 1927.

Sandburg, Carl. Abraham Lincoln: *The Prairie Years and the War Years.* New York: Harcourt Brace, 1989.

_____. *Lincoln's Devotional.* New York: Henry Holt & Co., 1995.

Simon, Paul. *Lincoln's Preparation for Greatness: The Illinois Legislative Years.* Champaign, Illinois: University of Illinois Press, 1990.

Slotkin, Richard. *Abe: A Novel about Abraham Lincoln's Youth.* New York: Henry Holt & Co., 2000.

Stephenson, Nathaniel (compiler). *The Autobiography of Abraham Lincoln: consisting of the Personal Portions of his Letters, Speeches, and Conversations.* New York: Blue Ribbon Books, 1926.

Stoddard, William Osborn, Burlingame, Michael (editor). *Inside the White House in War Times: Memoirs and Reports of Lincoln's Secretary.* Lincoln, Nebraska: University of Nebraska Press, 2000.

Temple, Wayne C. *Abraham Lincoln From Skeptic to Prophet.* Mahomet, Illinois: Mayhaven Publishing, 1995.

Thomas, Benjamin P. *Lincoln's New Salem.* Carbondale, Illinois: Southern Illinois University Press, 1987.

Walsh, John Evangelist. *The Shadows Rise: Abraham Lincoln and the Ann Rutledge Legend.* Champaign, Illinois: University of Illinois Press, 1993.

Wilson, Douglas L., Davis, Rodney O. (editors), Wilson, Terry. *Herndon's Informants: Letters, Interviews, and Statements About Abraham Lincoln.* Champaign, Illinois: University of Illinois Press, 1997.

Zall, Paul M. (editor). *Abe Lincoln Laughing: Humorous Anecdotes from Original Sources by and about Abraham Lincoln.* Knoxville, Tennessee: University of Tennessee Press, 1995.

_____(editor). *Lincoln on Lincoln.* Lexington, Kentucky: University Press of Kentucky, 1999.

•*Index*•

NOTE: Page numbers shown in **boldface** indicate photos of a person, event, or place.

•*Colophon*•

Abe Lincoln and the Frontier Folk of New Salem is set in the typeface Bell MT text, a computerized version of Bell Type. Bell is one of the roman typefaces classified as a transitional typeface. Transitional types were popularly used in the early 19th century, which includes the period of history covered in this book. The type considered by most authorities to represent the true beginning of the transitional form was that of John Baskerville. An amateur printer, Baskerville set up a printing office in Birmingham, England, about 1750 and introduced a number of technical innovations which affected the appearance of his typefaces. Baskerville's death in 1775 resulted in his types being copied, and their influence may be observed in several other English faces designed prior to 1800. One of these types is Bell, made for publisher John Bell in 1788 by the punch-cutter Richard Austin. Another example of a successful transitional typeface from that era is Bulmer, designed by William Martin for William Bulmer's Shakespeare Press. Baskerville, Bell and Bulmer typefaces are popularly used today for typesetting books.

—**Adapted from the book,**
***Printing Types: An Introduction*, by Alexander Lawson,**
published by Beacon Press in 1971